JESUS
-me and you-

D1352375

JESUS
—me and you—

by

CLIFF RICHARD
with Bill Latham

HODDER AND STOUGHTON

LONDON   SYDNEY   AUCKLAND   TORONTO

British Library Cataloguing in Publication Data

Richard, Cliff
  Jesus, me and you.
  1. Christian life
  I. Title   II. Latham, Bill
  248.4   BV4501.2

  ISBN 0-340-36931-0
  ISBN 0-340-36932-9 Pbk

First published 1985

Published by Hodder and Stoughton Children's Books,
a division of Hodder and Stoughton Ltd,
Mill Road, Dunton Green, Sevenoaks, Kent TN13 2YJ

Printed in Great Britain by T. J. Press (Padstow) Ltd, Padstow, Cornwall

Designed by Graham Marks

INTRODUCTION

If I said I loved you
what would you say?
If I said I needed you
would it frighten you away?
If I said I loved you
and I wanted you to be
my one and only lover
eternally.

Chorus
You and me and Jesus
Jesus, me and you;
on our own we'd break,
with Him we'll make it through.
Jesus, take us, make us
what you want us both to be;
I give myself to her,
she gives herself to me.

Love is really fragile
and if it's going to last
we've got to start by giving Jesus
future, present, past.
I ache the way I love you
but, babe, it's sink or swim
and when we look back years from now
we're gonna owe it all to Him.

Chorus
You and me and Jesus
Jesus, me and you;
on our own we'd break,
with Him we'll make it through.
Jesus, take us, make us
what you want us both to be;
I give myself to her,
she gives herself to me.

I really never thought there'd be a sequel, but the response to that first Bible selection in *You, Me, and Jesus* was so encouraging that here we go again.

I'm still conscious that my understanding of the Bible is relatively limited and that others would comment and explain far more expertly. All I can promise is that for over twenty years now I've been reading a chapter of the Bible more or less daily (admittedly sometimes late at night when I've been virtually clapped out) and I'm only too happy to grab the chance to pass on what's helped and challenged me.

In the first volume, I remember choosing parts of the Bible which focused on what Christians believe. Basic doctrines, you might say. This time I've put the emphasis more on how Christians should live. There's my opinion on each of the Ten Commandments, for instance. And I've hopped around Old and New Testaments quite a bit to unearth sound advice and good sense about tensions and problems that can knock all of us off-balance at some time or another.

There's no particularly logical sequence to the book, and you can dip into it at random or work through from the beginning. It may be an idea, if you aren't already following some daily pattern of Bible reading, to take just one section each day and use that to spark off your own thinking and study. Remember that what God says to you through the Bible verses is far more important than my paragraphs. I might be wrong. The Bible never is!

It's probably helpful, too, to have a Bible near at hand so you can read a little more of what comes before and after each extract. It's always better to see the Bible's teaching in its proper context — lifting out verses in isolation can sometimes be misleading.

Again I've used the New International Version. You may prefer another, but it's the version of the Bible I read at home. I find it clear, and gather from the scholars that it's a pretty accurate translation of the original.

I'd love to think that *Jesus, Me and You* might be helpful to some of you. In a lovely letter I received recently, I was thanked for 'inspiring people like us to ask when we don't understand'. Maybe what follows will help answer some of your questions. It may well raise others. If so, my Christian friends in Guildford would again be glad to hear from you if you need help. Their address is: 'Sayers', Mount Pleasant, Guildford, Surrey GU2 5HZ; but do enclose a stamped addressed envelope for a reply. Please understand that I cannot reply personally — it's just impossible.

Finally, thanks again to my spiritual leaning post, Bill Latham, without whom the book would never have happened; to Gill, for keeping the typewriter on the boil; and to Yvonne for not being afraid to criticise any woolly thinking.

See you at a concert maybe.

Cliff Richard

CONTENTS

HOW DO YOU KNOW?

On hearing his words, some of the people said, 'Surely this man is the Prophet.'

Others said, 'He is the Christ.'

Still others asked, 'How can the Christ come from Galilee? Does not the Scripture say that the Christ will come from David's family and from Bethlehem, the town where David lived?' Thus the people were divided because of Jesus. Some wanted to seize him, but no-one laid a hand on him.

John 7: 40-44

I'm very aware that people will come to this book with all sorts of different opinions, ideas and interpretations about Christianity and about Jesus in particular. As it says here, 'the people were divided because of Jesus'. They still are, after two thousand years. But be clear about this. I'm an authority on very little, and certainly nothing of much importance. I know a fair bit about making records, I don't mind admitting that, but, as I say, that isn't exactly a life-shattering accomplishment.

But the Christian faith isn't a matter of whether I'm an authority, or even whether I'm right. Rather, it rests one hundred per cent on whether Jesus spoke the truth and whether He was who He claimed to be. My Christian opinions and principles are not original and I can't take credit for them. I haven't concocted them from my own brain or from any flash of personal enlightenment. They're based, hopefully, as identically as possible, on the teaching and example of Jesus.

I'm often asked, 'How do you know *you're* right?' In all honesty, I don't! 'How do you know *Jesus* is right?' That's different, and I'm on much surer ground, where common sense blends with that abstract commodity called faith.

Apply the common-sense factor. Is there anything that Jesus said that you find inaccurate, daft, or irrelevant? Is there anything about Him as a person from the Bible's four biographies — Matthew, Mark, Luke and John — that you reckon is unpleasant or untrustworthy? Is there anything from historical or archaeological records that would cause a balanced or unprejudiced person to conclude that Jesus never really existed and was just a figment of someone's imagination? (In fact, there's more evidence for the existence of Jesus than there is for Julius Caesar.) And, with typical subtlety, a friend of mine said that if Jesus wasn't the Son of God, then His scriptwriter had to be!

I gather it was the writer C. S. Lewis who summed it up as follows: 'You can either dismiss Jesus as a liar or a madman, or fall at His feet and worship Him as Lord, but don't come to me with that patronising rubbish that He was just a good man. He doesn't leave that option open to us.'

When I first became a Christian, I believed that all Jesus said and stood for was true. I didn't know it in the sense that I could scientifically or tangibly prove it, but I believed it and my common sense told me it was not unreasonable. Now, after twenty years of living as a Christian, I've moved on a notch. Although I still can't scientifically or tangibly prove the reality of Jesus to anyone else, as far as I'm concerned I not only believe He's right — I *know* He is!

FORGIVEN!

The LORD is compassionate and gracious,
  slow to anger, abounding in love.
He will not always accuse,
  nor will he harbour his anger for ever;
he does not treat us as our sins deserve
  or repay us according to our iniquities.
For as high as the heavens are above the earth,
  so great is his love for those who fear him;
as far as the east is from the west,
  so far has he removed our transgressions from us.

Psalm 103:8-12

Among some really kind and encouraging reviews of *You, Me, and Jesus* was one that I have to admit upset me a bit. According to the writer, although I'd covered most of the basic Christian doctrines, there was insufficient emphasis on God's power to forgive.

Frankly, I just wonder how many pages he'd actually read because, of all the wonderful aspects of Christian truth, I guess it's my awareness of God's forgiveness above all else that motivates me to share Jesus wherever and whenever I can.

Nevertheless, just in case, let me set the balance right for that particular critic and, more especially, for anyone who thinks that their track record in life is too bad even to dare approach God. I know just how you feel but, in the light of the facts, our feelings can be misleading and even irrelevant.

The means of God's forgiveness — Christ's death on the cross, or the 'atonement', as theologians call it — is spelt out in the Bible in amazing detail. It's a plan that you see unfolding stage by stage from the beginning of the Old Testament right through until the gospel story in the New Testament. But, just for the minute, set aside the means, and focus on the plain fact that, whoever you are reading this page, God's love is greater than your sin, and His forgiveness and cleansing really are possible.

If you're at school and you've cheated your way through exams, God can forgive you. If you've lied or deceived or been unfaithful to someone you love, God can accept you as though you'd never done it. If there's something that has been on your conscience for years and it feels like some permanent stain on your life, God can wipe it clean, completely and for ever.

That's the difference between the quality of God's forgiveness and ours. When we forgive, it's very rare that we're able to forget as well. When God forgives there are no old scores that lurk on in the background, that one day might be dredged up to be settled. According to the Bible, it's as though our sin has been erased even from God's memory. Like the data on a computer, when the 'wipe' button is pressed it's gone for good, as though it had never even existed.

That's the quality of forgiveness that I know God has for me and, what's more, it's totally and absolutely undeserved. All I have to do is ask. That's why I want to serve Him better and love Him more. That's why I'm sad that I failed to communicate my own sense of gratitude effectively to at least one reader of *You, Me, and Jesus!*

THE ANSWER LIES IN THE SOIL!

Then Jesus said to them, 'Don't you understand this parable? How then will you understand any parable? The farmer sows the word. Some people are like seed along the path, where the word is sown. As soon as they hear it, Satan comes and takes away the word that was sown in them. Others, like seed sown on rocky places, hear the word and at once receive it with joy. But since they have no root, they last only a short time. When trouble or persecution comes because of the word, they quickly fall away. Still others, like seed sown among thorns, hear the word; but the worries of this life, the deceitfulness of wealth and the desires for other things come in and choke the word, making it unfruitful. Others, like seed sown on good soil, hear the word, accept it, and produce a crop — thirty, sixty or even a hundred times what was sown.'

Mark 4:13-20

I wonder if you're someone who 'went forward' at a Billy Graham or Luis Palau meeting a while back. Or maybe you responded to Jesus at some other smaller Christian meeting near to home or at a summer camp. If you did, maybe the question that's bothered you since is 'was it for real, and will it last?'

Sorry, but only you can answer the first of those. I know when I was on the platform at some of those fantastic '84 mission meetings, I could see that, among the thousands who came forward to commit their lives to Jesus, were some who weren't very serious. Maybe they wanted a better view of the speaker or of me, or just wanted to stretch their legs, but obviously they hadn't come for any vital life-changing reason.

Now obviously the people who did that — and I don't think there were many of them — would have forgotten all about it by now. It would be dismissed as just a bit of a laugh.

But what of the genuine ones? The people who honestly realised that they needed Christ to take over their lives and asked Him very simply to do it. Looking back now, you'll know whether it was real at the time and, if so, you'll be trusting the fact that it wasn't only something you did, but it was an action on God's part too. Because Christian conversion is a two-way contract — a commitment by you to Jesus, and by Jesus to you — it isn't a flimsy emotion that can 'wear off'. I know your side of the relationship can wear pretty thin from time to time, but there's no way there will ever be a cooling-off on God's part. Once you're in His family you're there for keeps, and when you look back years from now to that moment of conversion, the fact that it's lasted and marked a new beginning will prove the reality of it.

I have to look back over twenty years now to my first Christian commitment and, although it was the simplest, most undramatic of 'about-turns', I haven't the slightest doubt about its reality, because it has gone on and on, and got better and better.

So, as they'd say on *Gardeners' Question Time*, it all depends on your soil!

JUST A BEGINNING

So then, just as you received Christ Jesus as Lord, continue to live in him, rooted and built up in him, strengthened in the faith as you were taught, and overflowing with thankfulness.

See to it that no-one takes you captive through hollow and deceptive philosophy, which depends on human tradition and the basic principles of this world rather than on Christ.

For in Christ all the fulness of the Deity lives in bodily form, and you have been given fulness in Christ, who is the head over every power and authority.

Colossians 2:6-10

It can't be said too often or too loudly that becoming a Christian is only a start, and if you expect that initial act of commitment to solve all your worries then there's a good chance you're already pretty fed up and disillusioned with the whole Christian scene. Here comes the message, loud and clear again — originally for the Christians at Colossi — 'just as you received ... continue to live'.

Be clear about it now — Christian conversion is no magic potion to cure all ills. Receiving Jesus won't automatically solve your money problems, despite what the false teachers from America might promise. There's no guarantee against arthritis or headaches or cancer or heart attacks. It won't mean you're suddenly cocooned from the real world with its pain and suffering, its hunger and injustice. On the contrary — you'll be led right into it, because the real world is God's world, and that's where His people have to be — in the front line of action.

Sometimes I wonder what people expect when they become Christians, because in next to no time some of them complain that 'the feeling's worn off', or that life hasn't changed, or that 'things are just as difficult'. Maybe they think that beginning life with Jesus is like entering some spiritual Disneyland; you pay your money, go through the turnstile and from then on it's dreams come true — nasty, ugly things are gone for ever and all is spick and span and safe. Even the pirates are jolly, harmless characters, and the worst hazard is getting splashed!

Maybe preachers don't stress enough that the Christian life doesn't bring immunity from difficulty or pressure. And of course, when we first launch out as Christians, the Devil will make sure that all his heaviest artillery is set against us.

Forgive me for painting a gloomy picture but, in a couple of paragraphs, it's only possible to pinpoint one aspect of the whole. But, for some of you wavering Christians who can't understand why God hasn't stepped in and sorted out your particular mess, take heed of Paul's advice: 'just as you received ... continue to live'. Perhaps it isn't that God hasn't stepped in, but that you haven't stepped out.

INFLATED EGOS

If you have any encouragement from being united with Christ, if any comfort from his love, if any fellowship with the Spirit, if any tenderness and compassion, then make my joy complete by being like-minded, having the same love, being one in spirit and purpose. Do nothing out of selfish ambition or vain conceit, but in humility consider others better than yourselves. Each of you should look not only to your own interests, but also to the interests of others.
Philippians 2:1-4

Much of this book is about what Christians are like — or rather what they *should* be like! And, as I write, I'm conscious of how far short I fall from the target. Take this, for instance. Impressing *yourself* on others is what much of show-business is about, and I suspect, inevitably, my industry could boast more inflated egos than most. It's hard for the Christian entertainer to keep an accurate sense of proportion about his own importance. Not that selfishness and ruthless ambition belong only to show-business, I hasten to add. Far from it. 'Looking after number one' is an attitude that's wormed its way horribly into whole chunks of our society, and it's unhealthy and ugly and a far cry from Paul's teaching that we should consider others better than ourselves.

I find it odd and a little sad that critics often use exactly the reverse cliché when they want to knock; 'Christians,' they say, 'are all the same. They think they're better than anyone else.' In fact there's no room for a 'holier than thou' outlook and Christians, more than anyone, should recognise that they have precious little to boast about — at least, nothing that they can claim credit for. Everything they have by way of gifts and resources is God-given and, rather than encouraging some smug complacency, this should instil a more acute sense of responsibility.

And, before you retort that it's only natural to look after yourself, note that Paul doesn't say you shouldn't! '... look *not only* to your own interests,' he says. Care for yourself of course, but not at the expense, and with disregard, of others.

If you need reminding of the supreme example of humility, Paul goes on to give it in the verses which follow. They're worth looking up and reading.

A SUPREME STATEMENT

I eagerly expect and hope that I will in no way be ashamed, but will have sufficient courage so that now as always Christ will be exalted in my body, whether by life or by death. For to me, to live is Christ and to die is gain. If I am to go on living in the body, this will mean fruitful labour for me. Yet what shall I choose? I do not know! I am torn between the two: I desire to depart and be with Christ, which is better by far; but it is more necessary for you that I remain in the body.
Philippians 1:20-24

Forgive me for baring my soul a bit here, but these words have to be the ultimate, most marvellous summary of Christian faith, and I want so much to echo them. 'For me to live is Christ and to die is gain.'

In all honesty, I don't always feel like that, but Paul was wrapped up in Jesus so much that nothing else mattered. All he did was for Jesus and because of Jesus. Yet too often I catch myself with ulterior motives, lukewarm enthusiasm, and selfish priorities, and I know only too well that I still have a long way to go before I can put my hand on my heart and say, 'Me too. For me to live is Christ.'

Maybe it's a start, a crucial start, to *want* to be able to say it. Do you know what I mean? I can't hope that Jesus will be supreme in my life unless I desire Him to be. It's what John the Baptist meant, I guess, when he said that 'Jesus must increase, I must decrease'.

And then the other side of the coin — 'to die is gain'. Somehow I think I'm a bit further down the road on this one, because, just as I don't doubt the reality of God in my life now, I honestly don't have any doubt that God will be just as real in the life to come. My difficulty is that I enjoy life so much now that it's hard to imagine how it can actually get better! I know it will, and that's like some enormous future bonus. In the meantime, I can't pretend that I share Paul's dilemma and I'm more than grateful to go on living here and enjoying what God has given. Having said that, I know only too well that there are many Christians who don't have the privileges that I have, and life is tough and testing. Maybe one day I shall know something of practical and physical hardship, and life and death might take on a very different perspective.

Certainly I sympathise with Paul's problem. He was writing from prison and life wasn't exactly a load of laughs. He was confident that, after death, life quite literally would be heaven, and the prospect was marvellous. Humanly, he was tired and longed to be with his Father but, on the other hand, God still had work for him to accomplish and that was the end of argument.

Be encouraged by Paul's absolute certainty of what was to come, and remember that Jesus's own resurrection, together with His promises about eternity, were the basis of his confidence.

ACTION MAN

Do not merely listen to the word, and so deceive yourselves. Do what it says. Anyone who listens to the word but does not do what it says is like a man who looks at his face in a mirror and, after looking at himself, goes away and immediately forgets what he looks like. But the man who looks intently into the perfect law that gives freedom, and continues to do this, not forgetting what he has heard, but doing it — he will be blessed in what he does.

But someone will say, 'You have faith; I have deeds.'

Show me your faith without deeds, and I will show you my faith by what I do. You believe that there is one God. Good! Even the demons believe that — and shudder.

James 1:22-25; 2:18, 19

People mean well, but I really dislike that tag of being 'religious'. To me the word conjures up all sorts of negative ideas, quite apart from sounding so terribly boring. A friend of mine, who's a very active church leader, denies point-blank that he is the slightest bit religious — much to his congregation's confusion! The point he is making is that being religious or doing religious things doesn't count a jot as far as God is concerned. The Bible leaves us in no doubt that religious ritual, pious language, and church attendance add up to nothing when it comes to earning God's approval, and Jesus' scathing attack on those pillars of religiosity, the Pharisees, is the classic illustration. Hypocrites, whited sepulchres (or whitewashed tombs), and a brood of vipers, He called them. Obviously not Jesus' favourite people, yet so impeccably 'religious'.

The lesson James is reinforcing is short and simple. Religious trappings, words and theories are worthless unless there's a life style to match. There's only one way to demonstrate the reality of Christian faith and that's by being like Jesus in our behaviour, attitudes and relationships. In another verse, James puts it like this: 'faith by itself, if it is not accompanied by action, is dead'.

The bottom line when it comes to impressing people for Christ is not clever argument, catchy gospel songs, readable books, or well-promoted meetings. Those things help and God uses them, but in nine cases out of ten it's the way a Christian lives that speaks and challenges more than any spoken or written word.

When I first met a bunch of Christians way back in the '60s, we discussed and argued for hours on end about various Christian teachings. But what bugged me and caused all the chat was the way these people lived. They actually practised what they preached, and that was irresistible.

One of the greatest thrills for me each year is to see the crowds of people coming to my gospel concerts. 'Sold out' notices seem to go up in box offices as quickly, if not more so, as at my regular commercial gigs. Even more thrilling is to hear of people who are helped by these concerts to seriously think about the Christian faith, maybe for the first time. But I'm aware too of the thousands who come every year, who listen to what is said, probably agree with most of it, yet never allow Jesus to change their lives.

Sometimes it's good to be just a listener, but not all the time. 'Do not merely listen to the word...' says James. That's easy. 'Do what it says.' That makes all the difference!

BOO TO A GOOSE

For this reason I remind you to fan into flame the gift of God, which is in you through the laying on of my hands. For God did not give us a spirit of timidity, but a spirit of power, of love and of self-discipline.

So do not be ashamed to testify about our Lord, or ashamed of me his prisoner. But join with me in suffering for the gospel, by the power of God, who has saved us and called us to a holy life — not because of anything we have done but because of his own purpose and grace.

2 Timothy 1:6-9a

——————————

A friend of mine called Gerald Coates caused a stir a while back, accusing Christians of being 'too nice'. 'Far too many Christians are nice' he wrote, 'especially the so-called spiritual variety. A sugary existence, full of niceties and platitudes, devoid of gutsy laughter, radical honesty, humour and satire, criticism and judgment, will simply be sickly.'

Now Gerald's a bit of a one for 'coming on strong', and it's always unfair to take a quote out of its context, but sometimes exaggeration is a good way to make a point. Obviously it's better by far to be nice than nasty, but the 'niceness' Gerald was meaning was the sort of limp politeness that never wants to offend or upset or even challenge. There are times when we Christians have to do all those things, not with bullying aggression, but with loving concern.

The trouble is that we assume that a 'love' motivation and a gentle spirit — which I mention elsewhere — have to be demonstrated in quiet inoffensive behaviour, with the result that the Christian army sometimes presents itself as a bunch of timid little petals that daren't say boo to a goose. Well, you know what I mean!

It's easy to deceive ourselves, and our need to be 'nice' becomes just an excuse to avoid any spiritual confrontation or straight talking. We convince ourselves that it's better to be liked and say nothing than to speak out and risk a row. That's certainly not how Paul and the early Christians went

OH NO I'M NOT COMPLAINING —
I REALLY PREFER UNCOOKED FOOD!

about it. They knew only too well that they were in the front line of spiritual warfare and they went to jail for their faith, exhausted themselves for it, and were torn to shreds by lions for refusing to deny it. All through the centuries since, there have been Christians courageous enough to stand up to all that the opposition can throw at them, and today we inherit what they ensured was passed down. As Paul says, God didn't bring us into His family to make us feeble and timid, but rather to enable us to stand up on His behalf, come what may.

The chorus of a song called *Fighter*, which Sheila Walsh performs, says it perfectly:

'Where have all the Christian soldiers gone?
Where is the resistance? Will no-one be strong?
When will we stand up tall and straight,
Rise up and storm the gate?
How can we fail to get excited?
The battle is ours — why don't we fight it?
Battalions of darkness rise above me,
But God put a fighter in me!'

(Thanks to Graham Kendrick for the lyric.)

A BISHOP'S TRICK

Now, brothers, I want to remind you of the gospel I preached to you, which you received and on which you have taken your stand. By this gospel you are saved, if you hold firmly to the word I preached to you. Otherwise, you have believed in vain.

For what I received I passed on to you as of first importance: that Christ died for our sins according to the Scriptures, that he was buried, that he was raised on the third day according to the Scriptures, and that he appeared to Peter, and then to the Twelve. After that, he appeared to more than five hundred of the brothers at the same time, most of whom are still living, though some have fallen asleep. Then he appeared to James, then to all the apostles, and last of all he appeared to me also, as to one abnormally born.

For I am the least of the apostles and do not even deserve to be called an apostle, because I persecuted the church of God. But by the grace of God I am what I am, and his grace to me was not without effect.

If I fought wild beasts in Ephesus for merely human reasons, what have I gained? If the dead are not raised,
'Let us eat and drink,
for tomorrow we die.'

1 Corinthians 15:1-10a, 32

No excuses for returning to the subject of Jesus' resurrection. No doubt the row will have been forgotten by now, but one of our esteemed Establishment bishops recently put his foot in it by referring to the resurrection as 'a conjuring trick with bones'. To be fair to the bishop, he may have been misquoted — I know about newspaper fiction only too well — but nevertheless I suspect there are some churchmen, even teachers, who wouldn't be at all disturbed by the idea. Certainly a good deal of television time has been given over to theologians whose understanding of Christianity is significantly different to mine, and who make it as attractive and relevant as 'O' level algebra!

With respect to these learned men, please remember that without the Bible they have no more insight into the mind and working of God than anyone else in the world. Without the dependability and authority of the Bible, the only alternative is to create God in our own image. So He becomes a god that *we* can comprehend, who squares with *our* logic, and who can be contained within the boundaries of *our* understanding.

The bodily resurrection of Jesus according to the gospel writers is not reasonable, say some theologians, therefore it couldn't have happened. That's how they reason.

Do you see how crucial the authority of Scripture really is? If we deny its truth and accuracy, then we have nowhere to go for answers but inside our own heads. Personally, I have no problem in accepting the fact that God can and sometimes does intervene in human situations in ways that for us are impossible and miraculous. But, if He *is* the Creator and I am the creature,

then there's no problem. Obviously He is greater than I am, so I accept it and am just relieved and glad that He's still interested in us enough to bother.

Paul clearly believed that the bodily resurrection of Jesus really did happen. It wasn't merely a symbolic idea or cleverly conceived theory, but an event that actually occurred on a certain day at a certain time and in a certain place. Paul knew; he had seen Jesus, and the encounter had changed his life. Paul wasn't going to fight any wild beasts or face a jail sentence for any conjuring trick!

NO PROBLEM!

Hear and pay attention,
  do not be arrogant,
    for the LORD has spoken.
Give glory to the LORD your God
  before he brings the darkness,
  before your feet stumble
  on the darkening hills.
You hope for light,
  but he will turn it to thick darkness

and change it to deep gloom.
But if you do not listen,
  I will weep in secret
  because of your pride;
my eyes will weep bitterly,
  overflowing with tears,
  because the LORD'S flock will be
    taken captive.

Jeremiah 13: 15-17

Some of those late-night callers to radio 'phone-in programmes are so exasperating! I've just listened to one young lady who was telling the presenter how, for years, she had been addicted to first one drug, then another — heroin, cocaine, cannabis and Mogadon were all familiar to her — and she was explaining how each one had its own peculiar effects and pressures. Now she was struggling to free herself of the sleeping-pill habit.

It all sounded very tragic but my sympathy suddenly evaporated when the show's host asked her if she had any regrets. Without a hint of hesitation and with total conviction, she replied, 'Oh no, not a bit. It was all interesting experience!'

Frankly, I couldn't believe her, because I can't accept that anyone in their right mind would opt for a life totally influenced by and dependent on drugs. What I suspect is that the lady couldn't face up to the fact — and certainly wouldn't publicly admit — that she'd made a mistake. Her pride wouldn't allow it.

It seems to me that pride is one of those commodities that's either an asset in life or a gigantic hindrance. It's good and right that we have pride in our work, and for Christians it's natural and desirable that we're proud to be Jesus' people. It's even right to have pride in ourselves when we realise how valuable we are in God's eyes.

But this lady's pride was totally misplaced and sadly that seems such a common failing. Never own up to being wrong. Always *we* have to be right; to admit to a mistake is weakness. It's no new flaw; the Old Testament Jews were riddled with arrogance and pig-headedness, and the Lord was heartbroken by their stupidity.

In the 1980s, Christianity will make little sense to anyone until they admit that their past life has been anything but right. Sadly, all too often pride gets in the way and, like the drug addict, we lie to ourselves. 'No regrets, no problems', we say. Who do we kid?

QUITE A CONTORTIONIST

Endure hardship with us like a good soldier of Christ Jesus. No-one serving as a soldier gets involved in civilian affairs — he wants to please his commanding officer. Similarly, if anyone competes as an athlete, he does not receive the victor's crown unless he competes according to the rules. The hardworking farmer should be the first to receive a share of the crops.
2 Timothy 2:3-6

Best foot forward. Shoulder to the wheel. Nose to the grindstone. It all gets a bit confusing, what with soldiers, athletes and farmers! Paul, dare I say it, is obviously falling over backwards to make a point, and it doesn't need a genius to realise what it is.

The Christian life is no soft option, but a commitment that demands discipline, effort and hard work. They are the qualities that leap to mind from his three career illustrations.

The comparison with a soldier is often repeated in the New Testament and conjures up the idea of warfare, struggle and hardship. Hardly irresistible enticements into the faith — but then you can't accuse the Bible of misleading advertising! Taken seriously, Christianity is tough and costly, and we do well to weigh up what we're taking on when we enlist. But it's a soldier's obedience that Paul is singling out here. His duty is to follow and accept his officer's instructions and authority without question. Anything less means court-martial. The higher the degree of obedience and discipline of the individuals, the more effective the army is as a whole.

The parallel is obvious. If we choose to serve God, then we have to obey Him, and there's no room for divided loyalties. At school I remember singing that hymn, 'Like a mighty army moves the Church of God'. But does it? I'm not so sure. It would do if all its members were disciplined and obedient though. As it is, its progress seems at times more like a geriatric tortoise.

Then there's the athlete, who must compete according to the rules. Any infringement means disqualification and that's really tough after months of single-minded dedication and training. Is succeeding worth all the sweat and sacrifice? Ask the FA Cup winners when they bring the trophy back home, or the Olympic gold medallist doing his lap of honour, or even John McEnroe when he holds that cup aloft on the Centre Court at Wimbledon.

And, finally, the farmer's harvest is only achieved after months of early mornings and late nights, working in all weathers and in the worst of conditions. No cushy number.

Nor is being a Christian.

A CRUCIAL ENCOUNTER

In the year that King Uzziah died, I saw the LORD seated on a throne, high and exalted, and the train of his robe filled the temple. Above him were seraphs, each with six wings: With two wings they covered their faces, with two they covered their feet, and with two they were flying. And they were calling to one another:

'Holy, holy, holy is the LORD Almighty;

the whole earth is full of his glory.'
At the sound of their voices the doorposts and thresholds shook and the temple was filled with smoke.

'Woe to me!' I cried. 'I am ruined! For I am a man of unclean lips, and I live among a people of unclean lips, and my eyes have seen the King, the LORD Almighty.'

Then one of the seraphs flew to me with a live coal in his hand, which he had taken with tongs from the altar. With it he touched my mouth and said, 'See, this has touched your lips; your guilt is taken away and your sin atoned for.'

Then I heard the voice of the Lord saying, 'Whom shall I send? And who will go for us?'

And I said, 'Here am I. Send me!'

Isaiah 6:1-8

There are probably as many different conversion experiences as there are Christians and I only wish mine could have been half as dramatic as Isaiah's encounter with the Lord. It would certainly make a better story!

Now I'm not personally all that prone to visions or weird supernatural happenings, so exactly what it was that Isaiah experienced in the year King Uzziah died (whenever that was) I'm not sure. I doubt if I'd recognise a seraph if I bumped into one — although the six wings might be a bit of a give-away! But, strange and mystical though it was, I can accept without difficulty that on certain occasions throughout history God has shown Himself to people in extraordinary and profound ways.

Isaiah was one of those privileged to catch just a glimpse of God's greatness and majesty, and I imagine how he struggled for words to convey what must have been beyond his full comprehension. Whatever it was he saw, Isaiah felt absolutely wretched and unworthy. In the light of God's purity, the reality of his condition became clear for the first time. The gulf between his sin and God's goodness was too great. There was no hope, no

way he could ever approach a God so perfect.

And then, it seems, God gave to Isaiah a foretaste of what He was planning hundreds of years later when Jesus came and died as a sacrifice for our sin. At the angel's touch, Isaiah knew he was clean. It was as though he'd suddenly had a drenching hot bath and all the guilt and the dirt, everything that had blocked his path to God, had been washed away. He was forgiven, and he and God were at one.

Since Jesus came, God has had no need to use seraphs and burning coals to deal with our sin. The sacrifice was made once and for all at Calvary, but it's for us to realise it, accept it, and be thrilled by it.

Millions of others through the centuries have echoed Isaiah's response out of sheer relief, love and gratitude: 'Here am I. Send me!'

If you've never known the joy of the 'hot bath', and have never offered yourself to God in that way, then perhaps it's time you did.

LISTEN!

This is why I speak to them in parables.
Though seeing, they do not see;
though hearing, they do not hear or understand.
In them is fulfilled the prophecy of Isaiah:
'You will be ever hearing but never understanding;
you will be ever seeing but never perceiving.
For this people's heart has become calloused;
they hardly hear with their ears,
and they have closed their eyes.
Otherwise they might see with their eyes,
hear with their ears,
understand with their hearts
and turn, and I would heal them.'
But blessed are your eyes because they see,
and your ears because they hear.

Matthew 13:13-16

Something that causes the old hackles to rise — although hopefully they're well concealed — is the tendency for people to talk when they ought to be listening. It's a silly example, but I've often had to bite my lip when I'm all excited about a new record of mine, and I play it to someone for a constructive verdict. Instead of listening, they start twittering away after just a few bars, and it's evident that the music stops abruptly at the eardrums! They're hearing, sure enough — the volume level ensures that — but they're not listening. The ears are open but the mind's out for lunch!

I'm sure that's what Jesus meant when, far more politely, He quoted the Old Testament prophet Isaiah about 'hearing but never understanding' and 'they hardly hear with their ears'. It's nothing to do with being deaf or having limited brain power. It's just a refusal to think about what's being communicated. Now on a human level that needn't be any big deal. I might get upset but it really doesn't matter if people prefer to talk through my records (some folk have no taste!). On occasions it's even an advantage to be able to switch off from a barrage of noise and chatter, and free our minds to ponder something totally different.

What is vital is that we're alert enough to discern what's important and what's merely 'wallpaper' noise. When God wants to get through, it's time to listen! And, as I understand it, listening means clearing our minds of personal prejudices and wrongly-based assumptions, and applying our intelligence to sieving and assessing, as best and as honestly as we can.

I've said it many times before, but it frustrates me no end to know that people hear the Christian 'good news' but they seldom, if ever, genuinely listen to it. They're so mentally conditioned by misconceptions, ignorance of the facts, and social pressures, that what they hear is never allowed to penetrate.

If I'm frustrated by it, it must break God's heart.

IF ONLY ...

I rejoice greatly in the Lord that at last you have renewed your concern for me. Indeed, you have been concerned, but you had no opportunity to show it. I am not saying this because I am in need, for I have learned to be content whatever the circumstances. I know what it is to be in need, and I know what it is to have plenty. I have learned the secret of being content in any and every situation, whether well fed or hungry, whether living in plenty or in want. I can do everything through him who gives me strength.

Philippians 4:10-13

How many times do you catch yourself wondering how much better life would be 'if only...'? If only I had a different job ... If only I could fall in love and get married ... If only I'd never married and had my freedom again ... If only I were younger ... If only I were a bit older ... If only I could get out more ... If only I had more time ... If only things were different!

There must be so many people for whom life would be marvellous 'if only'. As it is, there's that one big drawback which sticks in our gullets and is the obstacle to real contentment and peace of mind. The truth of it is of course that, if that obstacle were suddenly and miraculously removed, it would only be a matter of time before another would take its place and we'd be back in our elusive make-believe 'if only' world.

If only we could be like Paul! How fantastic, even from a miserable prison, to be able to reassure his friends that he wasn't fretting or even upset, but that he'd learned to be content 'whatever the circumstances'. For most of us it's 'circumstances' that are the main determining factor in whether we are happy or not. If they're favourable and to our liking, then no problem. When there's money coming in and the family's well and the sun's shining, then great. When times are hard and someone's sick and the storms are threatening, then contentment so easily gives way to anxiety and gloom.

It's important not to confuse contentment with enjoyment. I don't believe Paul was sitting in jail with a soppy grin on his face, pretending to have a good time. There's no way he could have enjoyed being a prisoner. Nor does it mean an 'after Sunday lunch' sort of contentment, complete with heavy breathing and droopy eyelids! We know from other Bible reports that Paul was the last guy to accept, lazily or meekly, whatever came along. On the contrary, if a situation was unjust or evil, he was the first to speak out and fight to have it changed.

Again, don't confuse contentment with an Eastern sort of fatalism which, in the face of tragedy or persecution, shrugs its shoulders and says, 'It's the will of Allah'. Contentment is very different from apathy.

My understanding is that real contentment is being at peace with yourself — an absence, if you like, of that mental torture that produces anxiety, frustration and depression. For Paul, neither imprisonment nor hunger nor pain could disturb his peace of mind, because his heart was rooted in a person rather than in things or situations happening around him. Paul was content because he knew and trusted Jesus, and nothing that happened to his body, good or bad, could alter or undermine that relationship.

There were no 'if onlys' in the letter from Paul. His God was Lord of the 'here and now', however happy, tough or tragic that situation might be. And that was good enough for him.

WATCH OUT FOR THE LAW!

'Do not think that I have come to abolish the Law or the Prophets; I have not come to abolish them but to fulfil them. I tell you the truth, until heaven and earth disappear, not the smallest letter, not the least stroke of a pen, will by any means disappear from the Law until everything is accomplished. Anyone who breaks one of the least of these commandments and teaches others to do the same will be called least in the kingdom of heaven, but whoever practises and teaches these commands will be called great in the kingdom of heaven.'

Matthew 5:17-19

'Life's got enough rules and regulations as it is, without having to think about the Ten Commandments. Besides, that's all that Christianity is — don't do this and don't do that.' I bet you've heard that complaint before! I reckon it's cropped up, in one form or another, in virtually every school question-and-answer session I've ever taken part in. Of course it's a wrong and totally ill-informed criticism, although it's perfectly true that, for Christians, the Ten Commandments, or the essence of the Old Testament law, are still relevant. Although no longer the deciding factor in what makes a person a Christian, the Commandments weren't abolished by Jesus. Neither were they diluted, and they remain, it seems to me, as a sort of springboard for Christian behaviour. They're not the sum total, but certainly very much part and parcel of it.

For me it's totally reasonable and logical that God, the Creator, should give us some sort of blueprint or basic rules for living. With a new car or the latest computer gadget comes a set of instructions. If they're observed, great; if ignored, there's the inevitable breakdown. It's the same with the Commandments. We have the freedom to decide whether the Maker's rules are best, or whether we know better!

All ten of the Commandments concern relationships. The first four are about our relationships with God, the other six concern our relationships with each other. By and large it seems as though civilised society around the world has approved of the six and integrated them into their 'code of living', but has decided, in its dubious wisdom, that the four concerning God are outdated and best forgotten.

In the next ten segments I'm throwing out a few ideas about each Commandment, and why I reckon they're as valid in the 1980s as they were in Moses' day. After that, there's a bit about how Jesus made the Commandments even more perfect, what He meant by coming to 'fulfil the law', and after that, so you don't get too despondent, the most fantastic news ever!

GOD FIRST

And God spoke all these words:
'I am the LORD your God, who brought you out of Egypt, out of the land of slavery.
You shall have no other gods before me.'

Exodus 20:1-3

The chances are that most of us are in trouble from the start because the focus zooms straight in on our priorities. With no messing, God tells us that in everything He must come first. There must be no thing, no person, no relationship, no ambition, no career, no sport, nothing that topples God from first place in our lives.

In Moses' day, when the Commandments were first given, the Jews lived among many different tribes of people, all of them worshipping their own idea or concept of God. Sometimes the Jews were tempted to pray to, or even offer sacrifices to, some of these false, useless gods. Today the 'other gods' are not necessarily religious at all, and there are all sorts of things that compete for that all-important top spot in our lives. The greatest contender, of course, is 'I'. 'To heck with anyone or anything else — I'm going to do what I want.' I'm sure I'm not alone in thinking like that from time to time, and sadly I believe our society as a whole is often a very selfish one. But then, if we've evicted God — as our country has done to a great extent — it's inevitable, I guess, that we should make ourselves the pathetic successor.

The other contemporary god, needless to say, is materialism, which tells us that the object of living, or the yardstick for happiness and success, is wealth and prosperity. Bigger houses, faster cars, exotic holidays and so on. I know I'm the last one to appear to preach about that, because I have those things, but, in all honesty, what I can tell you is that they're not my gods. I had to decide, a good few years ago, which was more important to me — my career, which I love, together with all its rewards and demands; or my faith in God. Really, it was no contest. If I thought there was a reason that God would want me to serve Him in some other way, I'd move out and do it.

The question to ask yourself is who or what is worth your greatest allegiance, and, moreover, who or what actually gets it.

NO SUBSTITUTES

'You shall not make for yourself an idol in the form of anything in heaven above or on the earth beneath or in the waters below. You shall not bow down to them or worship them; for I, the LORD your God, am a jealous God, punishing the children for the sin of the fathers to the third and fourth generation of those who hate me, but showing love to thousands who love me and keep my commandments.'

Exodus 20:4-6

Here's a peculiar one for us, because the idea of bowing down to some idol or stone image is almost laughable. There probably is a danger that some Christians in distant parts of the world get hung up on old relics or man-made images, and superstition threatens to take over from commonsense and sound faith. But, by and large, I guess most of us don't bow down to little tin-pot idols in our bedrooms (hopefully not even Cliff Richard posters!), so does Commandment Two no longer apply?

I think it does, because hardly a week goes by without my reading in the newspaper about some tragedy or controversy emerging from one of the fashionable religious cults which seem to lure young people in particular into a realm of often unhealthy and antisocial influence. I'm thinking of groups like Hare Krishna, the Moonies, Scientology, or the latest guru with the unpronounceable name, who claims to have a monopoly on the latest divine insight but whose life is not dissimilar to a Las Vegas playboy's. I suppose it's partly the church that's to blame for failing to present Jesus with any relevance and dynamism, but I suspect too that there's a sort of anti-Establishment romance associated with these usually foreign-based and obscure teachings that have natural curiosity and adventure value.

It's worth noting that all these sects stem from man's attempts to find God. All of them are man-made and come from his imagination and brain. The Christian faith is the reverse; it's about God's initiative to find man, and the Bible helps us understand God's mind and His purpose for us.

Commandment Two is quite straightforward then. Even though they may appear more attractive, more convenient, more plausible even, the gods of the cults are to be ignored, whatever they are, and we are to reserve our worship exclusively for the God of the Bible, the God who loves us and longs that we should love Him in return.

OH BUDDHA!

I wonder why the names of other revered religious leaders are never used as swear-words. I've yet to hear someone yell 'Oh Mohammed!' or 'Oh Buddha!' when they've hit their thumb with a hammer. Seriously, it's strange, isn't it, that God's name and the name of Jesus Christ are used so often when we're angry or upset, almost as words of abuse or insult. I guess it's derived from our ancestors, who used more long-winded oaths and curses to express their emotion. 'By the blood of Jesus', they'd say, or 'In God's name'.

In a sense I can understand how that came to be, because it's part of perverse human nature to kick out at the things and people we love most when we're hurt or bad-tempered. You can see it when little children work up a tantrum and are really spiteful and cruel to their mums, even though a few minutes later anger gives way to kisses and cuddles.

What I find more difficult to stomach is the vocabulary that's laced with more references to 'God' and 'Jesus Christ' than the Archbishop would use in a fortnight! It's commonplace in my industry but it always jars. Maybe I'm too sensitive, you think, but what we say is invariably an expression of what we are, and a person who can use the name of Jesus mindlessly and carelessly is sure to have no respect and even less love for Him. You'll know how it is when you fall head over heels in love with someone. Even their name takes on a new and special significance, and the very sound of it makes you go weak at the knees!

It should be like that, but more so, when it comes to God and Jesus. Certainly the Jews held God's name in the strictest of reverence and, in a way I don't fully understand, the very name of Jesus itself has been vested with a unique power and influence. The disciples were instructed to perform wonders and miracles 'in the name of Jesus'. They were to pray to God 'in the name of Jesus', and we are told that one day 'at the name of Jesus every knee shall bow'.

I for one find the Lord's name far too important to devalue and throw away as a swear-word.

WHAT A DIFFERENCE A DAY MAKES

'Remember the Sabbath day by keeping it holy. Six days you shall labour and do all your work, but the seventh day is a Sabbath to the LORD your God. On it you shall not do any work, neither you, nor your son or daughter, nor your manservant or maidservant, nor your animals, nor the alien within your gates. For in six days the LORD made the heavens and the earth, the sea, and all that is in them, but he rested on the seventh day. Therefore the LORD blessed the Sabbath day and made it holy.'

Exodus 20:8-11

I don't know about you, but I love a good lie-in on Sunday mornings! Often, after a crazy week, I really feel I need it, and what a great moment when you wake up all dozy, and realise you can turn over again and carry on snoozing. And the way I understand this Commandment and what Jesus said about it hundreds of years afterwards makes me think that God doesn't necessarily mind one little bit. 'The Sabbath was made for man, not man for the Sabbath' are Jesus' famous words, and by that He meant that the day wasn't meant to be a drag or some kind of religious detention period. Quite the contrary. It's a day that has been set aside by God for our benefit and literally for our 'recreation' and, as I say, I can do with a fair old ration of that after the bombardment I get during the week.

It's a sort of recharging of batteries opportunity, and God knows far better than we do that that's necessary for us. During World War II, I gather, it was decided that, to step up factory output, workers would be required to man their machines seven days a week. Because of the war effort everyone was prepared to do it, but, after a trial period, the authorities found it just didn't work. Instead of output rising, it fell dramatically. Before long, staff were back to six days' work, with Sundays off. It was obvious that people needed that break in order to be at their best.

So the Sabbath, therefore, isn't intended to be a frantic religious dash from one church service to the next, and I know at least one bunch of Christians who hold their main worship and teaching service on a

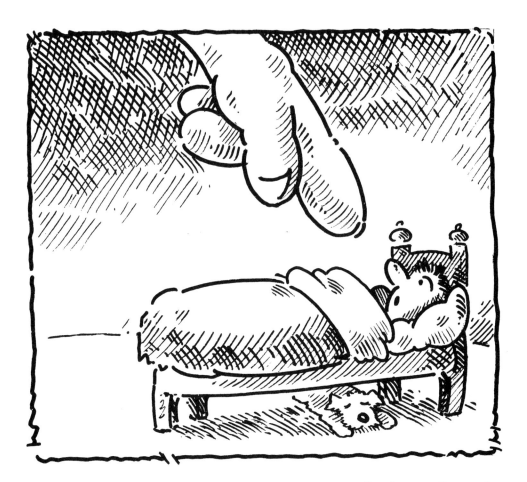

Thursday evening, so that families are free to enjoy Sunday together and perhaps, in a way, have even more time to thank God who provided this special day for them. There's a good deal of sense in that — although let me quickly add that I'm not suggesting church worship is unimportant. Far from it — and, to be honest, if I don't manage to make church any Sunday, I know I'm the loser. I've missed out, not only on what could be some crucial and badly-needed teaching, but also I've lost an opportunity for worship and fellowship with other members of the Family. They're vital components of 'growing up' as a Christian.

Just one extra thought; this is the only Commandment that's been actually altered since Moses received it, because, as we all know, Saturday is the actual Jewish Sabbath — the seventh day of the week. But the early Christians reckoned that they had something new to celebrate when Jesus rose from the dead on a Sunday, so that day took over as a sort of weekly anniversary, and that's certainly a fantastic reason for most Christian churches preferring Sunday services. As far as I know, there is just one Christian church — the Seventh Day Adventists — who believe it's right to still apply the Commandment as it stands, and consequently you'll find that their services and their 'separate' or holy day remain on the traditional Jewish Sabbath or Saturday. It goes to show how different we all are!

MUM AND DAD

*'Honour your father and your
mother, so that you may live long in
the land the LORD your God is giving
you.'*

Exodus 20:12

Something I read in the paper this week made my blood boil. In Sweden a father was fined, would you believe, for spanking his twelve-year-old son as a punishment for misbehaviour. Apparently the boy had actually gone to the police to report his father and, because of some so-called enlightened 'anti-spanking' law that Sweden has introduced, the police prosecuted. How mad can our world get? If it's now an offence for a father to correct his son with a good wallop if he thinks fit, then heaven help our future society. (And by 'a good wallop', incidentally, I don't mean uncontrolled, bad-tempered violence!) Certainly Sweden's new law isn't going to do much for Commandment Number Five for, instead of encouraging a strong family relationship, this man-made rule is surely going to foster division and mistrust.

OK, mercifully we have no such restriction in our country and I'm grateful to my dad, whose firmness and physical 'reminders' from time to time gave me an early grounding in what was right and wrong, acceptable and unacceptable.

One thing I envy about the Jews is their marvellous family loyalty. I'm sure they have their rows and bust-ups, just as all families do, but these seem to be invariably patched up and forgotten, and families remain united and dependent on each other. I'm sure it's because most Jewish parents are skilled in bringing up their children with the right blend of firmness and gentleness. A natural response to that is genuine love, respect and lifelong commitment.

It sounds pompous, I know — particularly for a single guy — to talk about strong families making strong nations, but I happen to believe it, and the impression I get is that when respect for parents is missing then respect for other sorts of authority goes haywire as well. What I'm saying is that it isn't the kids who are necessarily to blame. Irresponsible adult attitudes and daft 'grown-up' ideas don't always make for, or even deserve, honour and respect.

What I've said so far won't be much help to the boy or girl who finds it really difficult to respect one parent or the other because of their cruelty, bullying, drunkenness or whatever. All I can say is that, for good or bad, you remain the child of your parents and nothing will ever change that unique relationship. Your God-given responsibility is to honour them, even if you think they don't deserve it. At the very least they gave you life, and for that you owe them. It's for you, maybe with the help of a sympathetic school-teacher or youth leader, to work out how best you can practically honour them, and even practically love them, in the circumstances. Your commitment to them as a son or a daughter needs to be deeper and longer-lasting than theirs, maybe, has been to you.

WHODUNIT?

'You shall not murder.'

Exodus 20:13

Put the flags out — there's a Commandment here that most of us have kept (although they'll be down at half-mast when you realise how Jesus interpreted it!).

At first sight, 'You shall not murder' sounds straightforward enough, and it reminds us that human life is something precious and irreplaceable. We can't create life, so it follows that we have no right to take what we cannot give. Perhaps in Moses' time, murder wasn't considered quite the extreme crime that it is now, and even today, in some parts of the world, human life is comparatively cheap and expendable.

The positive aspect of the Commandment for me is that God must consider every human life really valuable. We matter to Him — your life as much as mine. We have to look to the New Testament of course, and to Jesus in particular, to discover just how much we matter.

Perhaps, however, the Commandment applies more widely than to just the obvious sordid murder, which all of us would condemn. What about its relevance to more complex issues, such as abortion and euthanasia? Here are far more difficult areas, not nearly as black and white as a criminal shooting or strangling! There's no way I would even attempt to give you absolute definitions of what is right and wrong in some of these emotionally charged situations because, to be quite honest, I don't always know myself. I can't begin, for instance, to condone the 'abortion on demand' principle. I find it's little more than a licence to kill, and totally abhorrent, but I sway to the other side of the argument and can only sympathise, for instance, with the twelve-year-old rape victim who is pregnant, and whose own physical and mental health is at risk if she has the baby.

It's a colossal debate of course, and I well appreciate that the demarcation lines are blurred. Euthanasia, too, throws up just as many uncertainties for me. As Christians though, we have to work out the answers as best we can, always remembering the one guiding principle; while we're free to form opinions, in the final analysis and in the light of the Bible's teaching, it's God's verdict that matters.

HANDS OFF!

'You shall not commit adultery.'
                              Exodus 20:14

———————

There's more about sex and relationships elsewhere in the book, so let's just focus on what's specified here — a husband or a wife being prohibited from having sex (or 'an affair', as we so delicately put it), with anyone other than their partner. Strictly then, for those of us who are single this may not seem immediately relevant, although, if we're anticipating marriage one day in the future, we'd do well to ensure that this direct and unambiguous Commandment becomes well and truly engrained.

I think it's important that we establish one crucial principle at the start. Nowhere in the Bible does it say that a sexual relationship between a man and a woman is wrong in itself. Just the opposite — we're told that sex is a gift from God, that it's good, and is to be enjoyed. So don't run away with the idea that the Bible is a killjoy when it comes to sex — far from it.

But where it does lay down very clear ground rules is about the context and circumstances of having sex; and, without exception, this is within a marriage relationship. We will have to accept that a large chunk of society will dismiss this as prudish and old-fashioned but, while not suggesting that it's easy and while I'm acutely aware of our own frailty, like it or not, this is God's way. And, in our more balanced honest moments, our hearts will tell us that there's a whole load of wisdom and commonsense behind it. It isn't a rule for rules' sake, but is to safeguard our happiness, health and peace of mind.

Adultery is wrong, not because the sex act is wrong, but because it undermines the security and permanence of marriage. As we have seen from the Commandment about loving parents, family structure is super-important in God's scheme of things. As well as causing pain and hurt, suspicion and guilt, adultery weakens and fragments families, and the ripple effect can be devastating for many more than the couple concerned.

What we too easily lose sight of is that marriage from God's perspective is even more than two people making promises and being committed to each other. It's about two people becoming one. That's all a bit mystical, I know, but it's a lovely concept which, if only husbands and wives remembered and accepted, would make adultery horrible and unthinkable treachery.

STOP, THIEF!

'You shall not steal.'

Exodus 20:15

Easy when it comes to burglary, breaking and entering, and million-pound wage grabs — it's just not on, other than for crooks and underworld villains. But, before giving yourself a self-righteous plus mark, what about that smart bit of fare-dodging on the bus, the unreturned library book, the hotel towel that looks much better in your bathroom, or the office stationery that's there for the taking? What about the bits and pieces from the supermarket, where sometimes the staff are so dozy and impolite that it serves them right if things are nicked from under their noses? And, as for the cunning bit of tax evasion, surely that's all par for the course! Everyone does it if they have any sense!

And I'll stick my neck out and say what about some of you Christians involved in the gospel music scene, who reckon that debts can be conveniently shelved or, even better, permanently ignored? I hear of more than the isolated instance of that happening and, if this particular cap fits, then I suggest you sit down with a concordance and a Bible, and check out the references to debts and debtors.

What we as a society have done is convince ourselves that some forms of dishonesty are more acceptable or forgivable than others. The criterion has become, 'If you can get away with it, all well and good'. After all, the government, the supermarket bosses, the business managers or whoever, can afford it, and there's no way they're likely to miss your trivial pickings.

It can get a trifle embarrassing, can't it, because this Commandment allows for no exception. Stealing is stealing, and the amount and the circumstances are irrelevant. All of it is dishonest and, in God's sight, stealing five minutes of your employer's time breaches the Commandment just as surely as the bank-robber's hold-up.

Have you ever thought what a fantastic community we would have if we could all trust one another one hundred per cent? Apart from saving a fortune on door-locks, security guards, alarm-bells and what have you, and as well as my being able to leave my wallet in the dressing-room without fear of it being whipped, what freedom and peace of mind we would all have! And that means another Commandment designed entirely for our good and benefit.

What it doesn't take into account is our natural rotten tendency to do wrong. That required a radical remedy, which God, in the book of Exodus, is just beginning to unfold.

'DID YOU HEAR ABOUT ...?'

'You shall not give false testimony
against your neighbour.'
Exodus 20:16

I could write a book about this one. 'Don't tell lies about other people,' God says. Or, if it isn't stretching it too far, 'Don't gossip!' I have a notion that we love to pick holes in others, because it's a load more comfortable spotlighting someone else's faults than focusing on our own. Besides, it does wonders for our self-righteousness. I'm afraid there's an unhappy tendency, even in some Christians, to indulge in gentle character assassination under the guise of that pious word 'sharing'. It's an immature Christian who gets his kicks from it, but we need to watch our motives very carefully. Pretending that we're having some constructive 'caring' chat about a 'friend' in the group or fellowship, it may be that we are indulging in nothing more than 'spiritual' gossip.

The Commandment, of course, refers to *false* testimony, and there are times when it's right and proper and genuinely caring for us to speak about someone else's difficulties, but only when we know for sure that we're talking about facts rather than rumour or speculation. There are two check questions which I reckon we should all ask ourselves before knocking someone's character. Firstly, am I absolutely sure it's true, and, secondly, even if it is true, is it necessary for me to say it?

An enormous amount of hurt and damage have been caused by wagging tongues. And James, in the New Testament, says that the tongue can determine the whole course of a person's life. 'With the tongue we praise our Lord and Father,' he writes, 'and with it we curse men, who have been made in God's likeness. Out of the same mouth come praise and cursing.'

I have to say, from my own experience at the receiving end, that the press have a good deal to answer for when it comes to spreading innuendo and lies. A while ago there was a story in a national newspaper with the headline 'SUE BARKER MOVES NEXT DOOR TO CLIFF — OFFICIAL'. In this instance the article wasn't particularly damaging but there wasn't a single grain of truth in it. Sue wasn't contemplating moving next door, or anywhere else come to that. Neither were the houses next door for sale. The whole story was total fabrication. The frightening thing is that this wasn't a rare isolated instance. It happens to me and to others time and again. Occasionally it is laughable; often it's personally offensive.

Maybe we should be praying for more Christian journalists to 'invade' Fleet Street, who would be more concerned for truth and less about gossip and fiction.

Isn't it lovely, by the way, when just occasionally you meet someone who isn't interested in people's failings — only in their strengths!

PREVENTIVE MEASURES

'You shall not covet your neighbour's house. You shall not covet your neighbour's wife, or his manservant or maidservant, his ox or donkey, or anything that belongs to your neighbour.'

Exodus 20:17

Straight to the heart of things, this one. An instruction for us not only to control our actions but our thoughts as well. Now we're getting into even more difficult territory!

Another word for coveting is desiring, and it's plain logic that if we could curb our desires, then acts such as theft and adultery would never happen. Inevitably one is the result of the other. I don't think we need to get too hot and bothered and guilt-ridden, by the way, about admiring other people's belongings. I've often gone into someone else's home and thought how great a picture would look on my wall, or how perfect that furniture would be for my studio. That's natural, surely, and we know from other parts of the Bible that God wants us to appreciate good things — and that even includes a pretty face!

There's a world of difference though in admiring a person's beauty and wanting it for yourself; or liking your schoolfriend's watch and wanting to own it personally. That sort of desire or longing is greedy, ugly, and the danger is that the wanting becomes so obsessive that our reasoning becomes twisted and a little voice within us says, 'Why shouldn't I have it? No-one will ever know.' And that's not far from the point of no return, where the thought becomes the deed.

One of the nastiest advertising slogans to be hurled at us was the one for a certain credit card which apparently could 'take the waiting out of wanting'. And there's an even nastier lyric of a pop song which says, 'if you want it, here it is, come and get it'. That's not God's way. His is quite the opposite and is summed up very simply in Hebrews 13, verse 5: '... be content with what you have,' says the writer. And, strange though it seems, that's even harder for the rich man than it is for the poor. The difference between contentment and healthy ambition is something I refer to elsewhere.

So that's the last of the Commandments. Now, let me guess your reaction. Your mind is saying what a fantastic world it would be if people kept them; your heart is telling you, 'I'd love to keep them but I'd never make it.' Right?

Thank goodness the Bible doesn't end there!

THAT TOUGH!

'For I tell you that unless your righteousness surpasses that of the Pharisees and the teachers of the law, you will certainly not enter the kingdom of heaven.

You have heard that it was said to the people long ago, "Do not murder, and anyone who murders will be subject to judgement." But I tell you that anyone who is angry with his brother will be subject to judgment.'

'You have heard that it was said, *"Do not commit adultery." But I tell you that anyone who looks at a woman lustfully has already committed adultery with her in his heart.'*

'You have heard that it was said, "Love your neighbour and hate your enemy." but I tell you, Love your enemies and pray for those who persecute you . . .'

'Be perfect, therefore, as your heavenly Father is perfect.'

Matthew 5:20-22a, 27, 28, 43, 44, 48

I can imagine the old disciples looking absolutely shattered when Jesus told them they had to do better than the Pharisees. The Pharisees, after all, were the top of the class when it came to observing the exact letter of the law. They knew the rule-book inside out and let everyone see it. Not only did they make a show of observing the Ten Commandments, but they were equally fussed about the thousand and one rules and regulations that were part of the Hebrew lifestyle. They were so religious it was almost awesome, yet here's Jesus telling His followers that they had to be better than these pious pillars of the synagogue. Unbelievable!

But Jesus began very slowly to unravel it for them. It wasn't that the law was to be replaced — far from it. It was simply that it hadn't gone far enough. It literally didn't go to the heart of the matter. It's not enough, says Jesus, for our behaviour to be right; our thoughts and our motives must be pure as well. From now on, the thought is as important as the deed, so that if I hate someone, it's as displeasing to God as if I'd murdered them. If I start thinking how good it would be to go to bed with someone else's wife, it's the same as if I'd committed adultery.

Now, before you dismiss all this an unreasonable and impossible, just think what Jesus was getting at. At the very beginning, God made man and woman perfect, and that's still His standard. He wants our hearts and our minds and our bodies to be in agreement with each other — not that we think one thing and do another, which is often what the Pharisees were like. They lived correctly but their hearts were mean and unkind. On one occasion Jesus called them 'whited sepulchres' (or 'whitewashed tombs') — all clean and spotless on the outside, but rotten and maggoty inside.

The Ten Commandments, Jesus said, are about what we do. God is equally concerned about why we do it and what we are. That sounds far more satisfactory to me.

If you've got a problem of keeping up with all this, by the way, I don't blame you — but there's more!

SOME SCHOOLMASTER!

Is the law, therefore, opposed to the promises of God? Absolutely not! For if a law had been given that could impart life, then righteousness would certainly have come by the law. But the Scripture declares that the whole world is a prisoner of sin, so that what was promised, being given through faith in Jesus Christ, might be given to those who believe.

Before this faith came, we were held prisoners by the law, locked up until faith should be revealed. So the law was put in charge to lead us to Christ that we might be justified by faith. Now that faith has come, we are no longer under the supervision of the law.

You are all sons of God through faith in Christ Jesus . . .

Galatians 3:21-26

So what sort of God is it that gives us rules we can't keep and makes demands we can't meet? It's all very well to say, 'Be perfect' but, if He seriously expects me to reach a standard like that, then He doesn't know much about me, for a start.

Well, puzzling though it may seem, God does expect that standard. In fact He requires it and He does know you inside out and back to front, and it's these few verses from one of Paul's letters that unravel the riddle. In the old Authorised Version of the Bible, verse 24 reads that the law was 'like a schoolmaster to bring us to Christ'. In other words, if your reaction to God's law is, 'Help, I can't keep it, I'm not good enough,' then full marks! That's exactly what the law is supposed to teach you — firmly and wisely, just like a good schoolmaster.

Think of it this way. God wants us to understand that He requires nothing less than perfection, so He makes that clear to us through the Old Testament law and through Jesus' new, even harder demands. At the same time, He knows only too well that, because of our natural tendency to do what is wrong — 'sin' is the Bible's word for it — we have no earthly chance of keeping those rules. So He offers us the one fantastic alternative — faith or trust in Jesus. Whereas the old system of law could only bring about a sense of failure and impending doom, the gospel (or the 'good news') introduced hope, new life and, most amazing of all, a 'not guilty' verdict from God for all our rule-breaking. That is what being 'justified by faith' means. In the Crusader Bible class I used to belong to, the leaders used to tell the kids that it was 'just-as-if-I'd' never sinned. I thought that was a useful way of understanding a difficult but vital Bible phrase.

So do you get the hang of it a bit? The law shows us what God's standard is, and it shows us how desperately we need Jesus to save us from the consequences of breaking it. If you still don't feel you need Him, it's unlikely you'll ever get to know Him.

GOD'S VERDICT

Therefore, there is now no condemnation for those who are in Christ Jesus, because through Christ Jesus the law of the Spirit of life set me free from the law of sin and death. For what the law was powerless to do in that it was weakened by the sinful nature, God did by sending his own Son in the likeness of sinful man to be a sin offering. And so he condemned sin in sinful man, in order that the righteous requirements of the law might be fully met in us, who do not live according to the sinful nature but according to the Spirit.

Romans 8:1-4

No apologies for going on a bit more about God's escape route! Here are a few more incredible verses which spell it out. If you ever wonder why Christians get fired up and enthusiastic about telling others about Jesus, then read this first verse over to yourself a couple of times. '...no condemnation to those who are in Christ Jesus'. No conditions, no 'maybe's'; it's a straightforward verdict and, if we were prisoners in the dock, we would be able, on the strength of it, to walk out, no longer in custody but free men or women, free boys or girls.

In *You, Me, and Jesus,* I tried to explain verse three and how, by dying on the cross, Jesus satisfied all the sacrificial demands of the law. Instead of you and me paying the penalty, He did.

There's a story told of an old habitual criminal who, throughout his life, had committed offence after offence. Finally he was brought before the judge, who happened to be his lifetime friend. Everyone in court wondered whether, because of their long relationship, the judge would be lenient. But when the time came for the sentence there were gasps all round when the judge announced that, because the law must be satisfied, he had no choice but to pass the most severe sentence possible. But then he added something else ... 'But, because you're my friend, I will pay the penalty instead of you. You may go free.'

Like most illustrations, it's far from perfect, but it gives a useful clue to what these verses teach us. Because He is the perfect judge, God has to see that the law is carried out but, because He also loves us just as perfectly, He sent Jesus to be our 'sin offering'.

Assuming then that we're concerned about living in a way that is acceptable to God — and I realise that there are some who couldn't give two hoots about that — there seem to be two options open to us. We can choose the Old Testament way — attempting to qualify by total unfailing obedience to the law (which, because of our nature, is impossible!) — or we accept God's free offer, which is wholly undeserved and could never be earned.

Just go back to verse one. Notice it isn't everyone who receives the 'no condemnation' verdict, but only those who are 'in Christ Jesus'. We need to be clear what that means and whether we are included!

COUNSEL FOR THE DEFENCE

My dear children, I write this to you so that you will not sin. But if anybody does sin, we have one who speaks to the Father in our defence — Jesus Christ, the Righteous One. He is the atoning sacrifice for our sins, and not only for ours but also for the sins of the whole world.

We know that we have come to know him if we obey his commands. The man who says, 'I know him,' but does not do what he commands is a liar, and the truth is not in him. But if anyone obeys his word, God's love is truly made complete in him. This is how we know we are in him: Whoever claims to live in him must walk as Jesus did.

1 John 2:1-6

Imagine a defence counsel who can guarantee us total acquittal on all charges. No matter how serious or dreadful the offence, the guarantee stands. No punishment, no stain on our character, not even an entry in the record books. Just total acquittal with no strings attached.

Unheard of, of course, in human courts of law, but that's just how it is in God's court, where day after day Jesus speaks to His Father on our behalf and in our defence. Don't you find that quite awesome?

The guarantee holds good, of course, because justice has already been satisfied. Our defence counsel not only pleads our case, but He's taken the punishment for all our wrong-doing as well. He did that effectively and finally by dying on the cross on that first Good Friday. So when Cliff Richard sins, Jesus doesn't ask His Father for yet another favour, but merely points to His scars and reminds God that the penalty is paid. Cliff is acquitted.

Too good to be true? Some think it is and, like those soldiers who refused to believe the war had ended and stayed holed up in their bunker for weeks afterwards, they miss out on what has to be the best and greatest good news ever offered.

But this passage should also impress those who see no need of Jesus. Folk who look at their lives and are either blind to their sin and wrong-doing, or are complacent about it and think it doesn't matter. Sin does matter. It's engrained in all of us, even in the most saintly of Christians, and anyone who claims otherwise has to be living in a five-star fool's paradise.

It's ironic that scoffers and doubters often label Christians as goody-goodies. Actually it's Christians who have recognised and owned up to the fact that they're 'baddy-baddies'. And, much as they'd love to give their heavenly defence counsel a rest, they need Him to plead their cause day after day after day.

I have to admit that autographs can be a bit of a bind, but most times I grin and bear it . . .
Hanne Jordan

. . . even when it's perishing cold! *Hanne Jordan*

A brisk walk over the golf course with the dogs is much better for the circulation.
Bill Latham

But better still is a thrash around the tennis court – a game I've come to love over recent years. Here BBC commentator, Gerry Williams, has a word across the net at my annual Pro-Celebrity Tournament at Brighton.

Hanne Jordan

The old gang – The Shadows – Brian, Hank and Bruce – during our 25th anniversary concerts.

Hanne Jordan

Bill Latham and I have travelled a good few thousand miles over the years to Tear Fund projects in faraway places.

Bill Latham

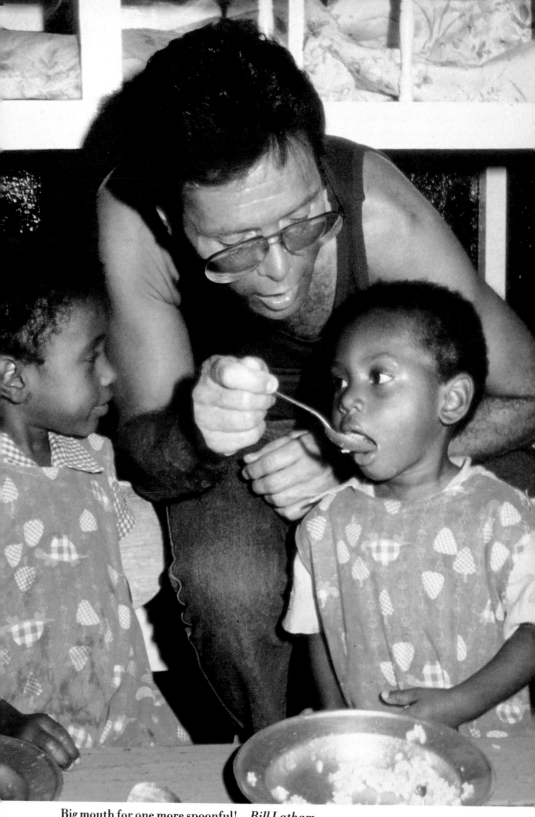

Big mouth for one more spoonful! *Bill Latham*

It's amazing what furniture people have in their gardens these days!   *Hanne Jordan*

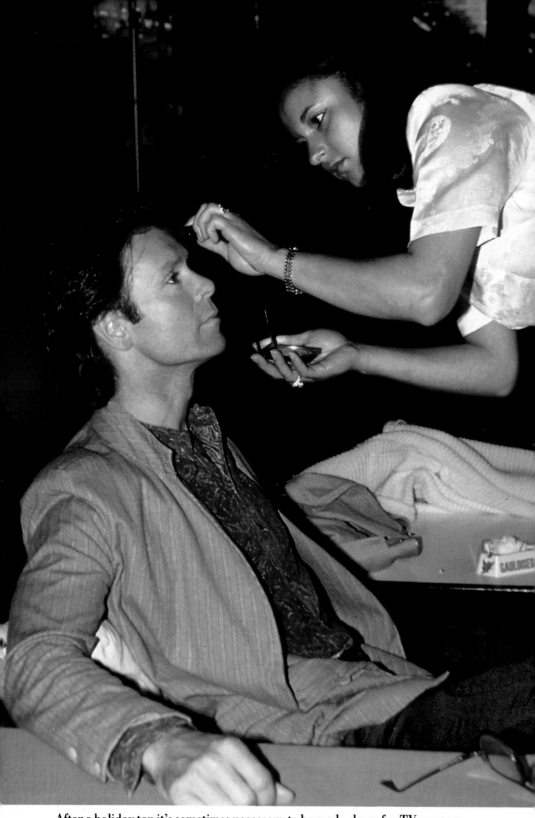

After a holiday tan it's sometimes necessary to be made-down for TV cameras, rather than made-up!

Hanne Jordan

You couldn't perform with dramatic laser lighting like this in the old days. There's no way I'd want to turn the clock back.   *Hanne Jordan*

Hanne Jordan

Taking part in large-scale mission meetings is always a special thrill for me. The two dots on the platform are me and Sheila Walsh singing at Luis Palau's rally at QPR football stadium in London.   *Hanne Jordan*

A nervous moment just before going on-stage at Greenbelt. Checking his watch is compère Garth Hewitt.   *Hanne Jordan*

Two special and memorable moments for me on early Tear Fund trips were visiting Mother Teresa and the Sisters of Charity at their base in Calcutta (George Hoffman and Bill Latham were with me)

and seeing the plight of children in Bangladesh refugee camps.　　*Bill Latham*

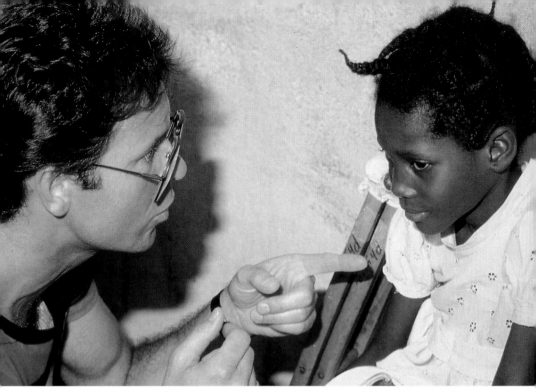

The vulnerability of children in needy Third World countries demands a special compassion from all of us.   *Bill Latham*

So what's the joke? It's what every fashionable guy wears in Haiti!   *Bill Latham*

It was fun being part of BBC TV's 'Rock Gospel Show'. Alvin Stardust is making a point during rehearsal with the Show's host, Sheila Walsh. *Hanne Jordan*

Add some laser beams and a puff of smoke to regular stage lighting and you can produce some stunning – and expensive – effects! *Hanne Jordan*

JUST DESERTS

Do not be deceived: God cannot be mocked. A man reaps what he sows. The one who sows to please his sinful nature, from that nature will reap destruction; the one who sows to please the Spirit, from the Spirit will reap eternal life. Let us not become weary in doing good, for at the proper time we will reap a harvest if we do not give up. Therefore, as we have opportunity, let us do good to all people, especially to those who belong to the family of believers.

Galatians 6:7-10

It sounds so old-fashioned in our 'anything goes' days to trot out the old idea of reaping what we sow. Some would say that just isn't true and you only need glance at the newspapers to realise that intentionally evil men get away with their wickedness, while seemingly good people end up the victims. In an unjust world, the concept of just deserts is hard to believe.

Yet according to the Bible, unfashionable or not, difficult to accept or not, the principle stands. No one fools God. The person who lives to please himself and lifts two fingers to God and to other people will not get away with it. It's plain and unambiguous, and the warning rings out; 'Don't be deceived!'

Think for a minute. While evil men may seem to prosper in this life, I wonder in reality how many of them really do. I don't mean superficially or materially — we're so easily taken in by appearances — but how many are better off in themselves and more inwardly at peace or more genuinely happy. I don't mean that to sound glib, but everyone who has seen through the illusion of wealth or sexual promiscuity will know and agree that what we are within matters more than what we own or do.

Evil isn't prospering when the evil-doer is secretly lonely, embittered and guilt-ridden, even if he is lounging by a private pool, surrounded by extrovert company, and has a Rolls in the garage. Conversely, good isn't defeated when a serene, loving and quietly confident spirit radiates from a body that is crippled or deprived.

But there's a bigger perspective. Paul doesn't teach that the reaping will happen in this life, but rather at a later stage, after physical death. The two alternatives are stark and sober, and they don't need my embroidery.

Meanwhile, the warning is plain. If you think you can get away with it, whatever 'it' may be, well, perhaps you can as far as other folk are concerned, but 'do not be deceived: God cannot be mocked'.

FACE VALUE

Once more he visited Cana in Galilee, where he had turned the water into wine. And there was a certain royal official whose son lay sick at Capernaum. When this man heard that Jesus had arrived in Galilee from Judea, he went to him and begged him to come and heal his son, who was close to death.

'Unless you people see miraculous signs and wonders,' Jesus told him, 'you will never believe.'

The royal official said, 'Sir, come down before my child dies.'

Jesus replied, 'You may go. Your son will live.'

The man took Jesus at his word and departed. While he was still on the way, his servants met him with the news that his boy was living. When he enquired as to the time when his son got better, they said to him, 'The fever left him yesterday at the seventh hour.'

Then the father realised that this was the exact time at which Jesus had said to him, 'Your son will live.' So he and all his household believed.

John 4:46-53

Sometimes when I read the Bible, just one word or one phrase will leap out with special impact and provide some new insight or challenge. This story is a case in point. I don't know how often I've read it before, but this time what struck home was that the man 'took Jesus at His word'. I never noticed that in the past or, if I did, it never registered.

It wouldn't have been surprising if this presumably intelligent royal official had stopped and argued. He obviously believed Jesus had special healing powers or he would never have requested Him to come in the first place. But to his way of thinking Jesus had to visit personally. It only made sense if Jesus could see for Himself his boy's condition. Only then could He do what was necessary. Yet when Jesus instructed him to go home alone, telling him that his son would live, the man 'took Jesus at His word and departed'.

I wonder how you and I would have reacted. I'd like to think I'd have done the same with as little hesitation, but I'm not sure. I'd possibly think I knew better. I'd know how seriously ill the boy was, because I'd seen him. Jesus hadn't. I knew that Jesus had touched people before and they were healed. That's the way He did it. He had to be there in person and touch them. It didn't make sense for Him to be a few miles away. It didn't add up. It wasn't logical. What if Jesus had got it wrong? Perhaps He was tired…

Yet, however impossible it seemed, however little he understood, the official took Jesus at His word. What a lesson in faith! While we'd be looking dubious and asking for explanations, the father was home with his son, rejoicing and thanking God for His goodness.

So often we miss out on God's blessing, I believe, because we don't honestly take Him at His word. We say we do, but when it comes to the crunch we hold back. We don't pray as we should because our human reason tells us God can't answer. We don't go where God leads because logic tells us it's stupid. We don't live dangerously as He directs because we doubt His ability to look after us.

Just imagine what an impact the church would have if, instead of all of us cautious, hesitant disciples, there was an army of people who, like the official, recognised Jesus' authority and took Him at His word and stepped out.

GOOD FOR NOTHING?

*Just as each of us has one body with
many members, and these members do
not all have the same function, so in
Christ we who are many form one
body, and each member belongs to all
the others. We have different gifts,
according to the grace given us. If a
man's gift is prophesying, let him use
it in proportion to his faith. If it is
serving, let him serve; if it is teaching,
let him teach; if it is encouraging, let
him encourage; if it is contributing to
the needs of others, let him give
generously; if it is leadership, let him
govern diligently; if it is showing
mercy, let him do it cheerfully.*

Romans 12:4-8

I'm positive that the Christians who please God the most are often those
who do the most mundane and 'unglamorous' jobs. There's a danger that
'public Christians', like myself, unwittingly set a sort of inaccurate and
unhelpful example in terms of what's important.

As most people know, I have enormous respect for Dr Billy Graham.
Humanly speaking, I guess he has contributed more to church growth in
this world than any other single man over the past few decades. But, as I'm
sure Billy would be the first to say, from God's perspective his contribution
or 'ministry' is no more important and no more acceptable than the
committed and dependable caring that a group of young Christians, for
instance, might show towards a lonely and frail old lady. The kind of job we
do is not what counts. We're not all suddenly to leap into the nearest pulpit
or on to the largest platform and become 'personalities'. Heaven forbid!
Believe me, I reckon that the personality aura can be a positive hindrance
when it comes to pointing people away from ourselves to Jesus. Sometimes
when I'm talking about Jesus at a meeting, I inwardly groan when someone
reckons that snapping a photo of Cliff Richard is more important, and is
apparently oblivious to all I've said.

Never let the Devil trap you into thinking that, because you could never
in a million years stand up and speak to an audience, you're therefore
potentially less useful. That's just not true, and we need to realise again that
God's measurements are quite different from the worldly ones we apply.
We're conditioned to equate success with bigness or large numbers or
public impact, but God sees it from another angle. He isn't looking for a
spectacular performance, not even an impressive one. What He longs for
from you and me is that we're obedient to whatever He gives us to do.

Now don't misunderstand me -- I'm not suggesting for one minute that Christians are excused all responsibility. To my mind there are too many already who occupy the church pews but do precious little to reflect God's love to others. Young Christians in particular need to be cautious about packing their diaries with festivals, conferences and gospel concerts. All intake and no output makes for bloated, lazy people. Sure, there are times to watch and listen and enjoy, but it's evident from these few verses alone that Christianity is about doing. It's a life style for the practical, not a cop-out for the dreamers.

The point is that, whoever you are and whatever your age or circumstances, there is a role for you in the Christian family, which is important and which is your role and yours only. It may be to befriend and pray for just one individual, year after year. It may be to put away chairs at the church fellowship meeting. It may be to visit an elderly or disabled person. It may be to be a flickering little light in an office which otherwise would be in permanent spiritual black-out.

God isn't going to lead you into doing anything you won't enjoy or that's not 'you'. Quite the contrary -- but when He leads you must be disciple enough to follow!

WINGS OF EAGLES

Do you not know?
Have you not heard?
The LORD is the everlasting God,
the Creator of the ends of the earth.
He will not grow tired or weary,
and his understanding no-one can
fathom.
He gives strength to the weary
and increases the power of the weak.
Even youths grow tired and weary,

and young men stumble and fall;
but those who hope in the LORD
will renew their strength.
They will soar on wings like eagles;
they will run and not grow weary,
they will walk and not be faint.

Isaiah 40:28-31

There are times when I look in the mirror and groan. Instead of the 'Peter Pan of Pop', it's more like his grandad looking back at me! All of us know what it's like to be totally clapped out and I'm no exception. The difference is that in my job I mustn't show it!

There's no shame attached to being physically tired, but I reckon Isaiah was thinking more of that state of mind when everything is just too much bother. We know what we ought to do but the enthusiasm we once had seems to have worn thin, and it's tempting just to opt out and let someone else make the effort.

Strangely enough, some of my best, most rewarding times have been when I've had to combat those moods. I'm thinking particularly of when it's been Christian meetings or responsibilities that I've wanted to shirk. The other Sunday, for instance, towards the end of an overseas tour, I was scheduled to take part in a 9.00 a.m. church service and, after a really late night, it was the last thing I wanted. After a few groans and grumbles, and muttering solemn doubts about the sanity of the organisers, I gritted my teeth and got on with it. I should have known better of course, for it turned out fantastically. The highlight of the tour, no less, and a real spiritual tonic.

It wasn't that the tiredness disappeared. I was short of sleep and nothing would change that. But somehow, as I've experienced dozens of times before, I was sort of buoyed up by the occasion and it was all strangely effortless. I can relate it exactly to Isaiah's picture of the eagles' wings, and that graceful, effortless flight. No frantic flapping to get under way or make progress, but stable and somehow powerful on invisible currents of air.

Isaiah promises a source of strength to help us soar above trying situations and circumstances, and I often quote that New Testament principle of God's strength showing up best in weak people. I shouldn't really be surprised, after all these years, to discover that it's actually true!

THE FACTS OF LIFE

This is the message we have heard from him and declare to you: God is light; in him there is no darkness at all. If we claim to have fellowship with him yet walk in the darkness, we lie and do not live by the truth. But if we walk in the light, as he is in the light, we have fellowship with one another, and the blood of Jesus, his Son, purifies us from every sin. If we claim to be without sin, we deceive ourselves and the truth is not in us. If we confess our sins, he is faithful and just and will forgive us our sins and purify us from all unrighteousness. If we claim we have not sinned, we make him out to be a liar and his word has no place in our lives.

1 John 1:5-10

'The heart of the problem,' I remember someone saying, 'is the problem of the human heart.' And, after our refresher course on the Ten Commandments, it would take a peculiar person to disagree. Forget the lie about Christians thinking they're better than other folk. In fact it's the exact reverse. Christians begin by admitting to themselves and confessing before God that they are as bad, and often a darn sight worse, than other folk! Check back on the Commandments again if you need to, and you'll see that we have a natural tendency or a built-in bias to ignore them and disobey them, even though our better judgment tells us they're good and sensible.

'If you claim to be without sin, who are you kidding?' reads the Cliff version of verse eight. Certainly not me — and, even more certainly, not God.

Sin is a fact of life. We inherit it, and it gets in the way and spoils and destroys. It makes ugly what is potentially lovely.

Personally, that's why I consider protests and rallies, demonstrations and petitions against this and that, although well-intentioned and sometimes useful, really only scratch the surface of what is wrong. It's only when our hearts are changed that evil behaviour and oppressive attitudes will be eradicated. 'Communism would put a new suit on that man,' said the Marxist to a Christian about a scruffy old tramp. 'That may be,' came the answer, 'but Jesus would put a new man in that suit!'

Of course Christianity doesn't leave us wallowing in futility and hopelessness. The magnificent news here is that Jesus is available, not only with forgiveness, but with authority to purify us and cleanse us in God's sight. What beautiful reassuring verses for anyone who feels too ashamed or unworthy even to whisper a prayer to God. On the strength of this, we can be one hundred per cent sure that, no matter how rotten or dreadful our past, a complete wiping of the slate and a new start really are possible.

LAST BUT NOT LEAST

Then he consecrated Jesse and his sons and invited them to the sacrifice.

When they arrived, Samuel saw Eliab and thought, 'Surely the LORD's anointed stands here before the LORD.'

But the LORD said to Samuel, 'Do not consider his appearance or his height, for I have rejected him. The LORD does not look at the things man looks at. Man looks at the outward appearance, but the LORD looks at the heart.'

Then Jesse called Abinadab and made him pass in front of Samuel. But Samuel said, 'The LORD has not chosen this one either.' Jesse then made Shammah pass by, but Samuel said, 'Nor has the LORD chosen this one.' Jesse made seven of his sons pass before Samuel, but Samuel said to him, 'The LORD has not chosen these.' So he asked Jesse, 'Are these all the sons you have?'

'There is still the youngest,' Jesse answered, 'but he is tending the sheep.'

Samuel said, 'Send for him; we will not sit down until he arrives.'

So he sent and had him brought in. He was ruddy with a fine appearance and handsome features.

Then the LORD said, 'Rise and anoint him; he is the one.'

1 Samuel 16: 5b-12

Here's a shot in the arm for anyone who rules out their usefulness to God because of a poor job or a puny physique. In Old Testament days, the youngest of the family was invariably the last in line for responsibility. He was the one who was lumbered with the chores that were too mucky or mundane for his elder brothers. Being the youngest meant being at the bottom of the pile. Life was tough. And even Samuel, one of God's Old Testament 'greats', jumped to wrong conclusions.

He'd come to discern which of Jesse's eight sons was to take over from Saul as king of Israel, and he was taken in by first impressions and by what society said was important. Obviously it had to be the eldest. Social respect, maturity, experience, poise. Surely this was the guy.

Sorry, Samuel, try again!

Well, it had to be the second eldest — or the third — or the fourth .... But the kid brother — that was ridiculous! He hadn't washed, let alone dressed up to impress.

'So what?' Samuel heard. 'That's my man!'

What Samuel learned from this almost Monty Python type of encounter, and what we find so hard to get into our heads, is that outward appearance and all those things that count for so much socially aren't even listed in God's assets column. Good looks, intelligence, success, wealth, outgoing personality and the rest may well be the passport to social climbing, but not to God's approval. Happily He sees beyond superficial and often misleading facades, straight to motives and priorities. A lousy job — or no job at all, a dumpy figure, or a quiet personality, are irrelevant. The one qualification He looks for is a willingness to tackle whatever responsibility He gives.

Some of the most impressive and fantastic Christians I've met wouldn't be given a second look by the world. I promise you, it's the world's loss!

KEEP YOUR HAIR ON!

But mark this: There will be terrible times in the last days. People will be lovers of themselves, lovers of money, boastful, proud, abusive, disobedient to their parents, ungrateful, unholy, without love, unforgiving, slanderous, without self-control, brutal, not lovers of the good, treacherous, rash, conceited, lovers of pleasure rather than lovers of God -- having a form of godliness but denying its power. Have nothing to do with them.

For the time will come when men will not put up with sound doctrine. Instead, to suit their own desires, they will gather around them a great number of teachers to say what their itching ears want to hear. They will turn their ears away from the truth and turn aside to myths. But you, keep your head in all situations ...

2 Timothy 3: 1-5; 4: 3-5a

It's a gloomy picture this, but a shot across the bows for those who believe that we humans are slowly evolving into altogether better, more superior people. Personally I can't see the evidence of it. Without wanting to appear a misery-guts, I reckon that if you brought some alien into your home for a few weeks, sat him down in front of the telly, and supplied him with all the daily newspapers, his impression of our society wouldn't be far different from Paul's description.

Of course it's a generalisation, and good, kind and well-intentioned people are still around. But considering these words were written nearly two thousand years ago, they reflect with uncanny accuracy what seems to be surfacing all around us.

I expect the humanists won't agree, but I believe that, if as a society we abandon God as a foolish and old-fashioned superstition, then the only logical alternative is to eat, drink and be merry, for tomorrow we die. Why bother to make an effort to please anyone other than ourselves if life has no rules, no purpose, and no creator? If it was by accident we began, then life itself is little more than a gamble and the only restraint on our behaviour is self-preservation.

As I say, it's dismal reading, and it's for you to decide whether these tendencies are on the increase or whether it's just a jaundiced sign of middle age! If you're inclined to agree though, be sure to grasp the point of it all. A situation like this is the sign that the Lord's second coming is not that far away.

JESUS IS LORD

Your attitude should be the same as that of Christ Jesus:
Who, being in very nature God,
    did not consider equality with God something to be grasped,
but made himself nothing,
    taking the very nature of a servant,
    being made in human likeness.
And being found in appearance as a man,
    he humbled himself
    and became obedient to death — even death on a cross!
Therefore God exalted him to the highest place
    and gave him the name that is above every name,
that at the name of Jesus every knee should bow,
    in heaven and on earth and under the earth,
and every tongue confess that Jesus Christ is Lord,
    to the glory of God the Father.

Philippians 2: 5-11

If ever there was someone who had complete justification for throwing His weight around, it was Jesus. As God's Son and the one who set the universe in motion, He could have blitzed our world into terrified submission. Like the absentee owner of some giant workforce, he could have arrived with trumpets blowing, demanding the ultimate in VIP respect.

But that's not our God. His way was a stable for a birthplace, simple peasant folk for parents, carpentry for a trade, fishermen and taxmen for friends. He cried with concern and disappointment over people's hardness, and exhausted Himself with three years of constant travel and ministry. He made do with the bare essentials for living and when He died, with no property or estate to leave behind, He was spat at and jeered, and discarded as the lowest of the low. That's how much Jesus humbled Himself, and it's just a tiny fraction of that humility that's required of His followers.

One day it will be different. Then it will be Jesus, the King of Kings, before whom everyone — literally everyone who has ever lived — will have to bow. Outstanding, selfless Christians will be there, who will have given their lives in the service of others. So too will the scoffers and the cynics, and the evil people who have chosen to serve darkness rather than light. And the 'don't knows' will be there too.

On that day there'll be no doubts. It will be unanimous acclaim. 'Jesus Christ is Lord!' Tragically, for some the discovery will be too late.

LIKE A THIEF

For the Lord himself will come down from heaven, with a loud command, with the voice to the archangel and with the trumpet call of God, and the dead in Christ will rise first. After that, we who are still alive and are left will be caught up with them in the clouds to meet the Lord in the air. And so we will be with the Lord for ever. Therefore encourage each other with these words.

Now, brothers, about times and dates we do not need to write to you, for you know very well that the day of the Lord will come like a thief in the night. While people are saying, 'Peace and safety,' destruction will come on them suddenly, as labour pains on a pregnant woman, and they will not escape.

But you, brothers, are not in darkness so that this day should surprise you like a thief. You are all sons of the light and sons of the day. We do not belong to the night or to the darkness. So then, let us not be like others, who are asleep, but let us be alert and self-controlled.

1 Thessalonians 4: 16-5: 6

Those who have seen me in concert over recent years will know that one of my favourite performance numbers is a song called *Thief in the Night*. We use lasers, great mushrooms of smoke and some fantastic lighting effects, and visually it's stunning. I often wish I could be out in the audience watching!

But I wonder too how many people who have heard that song realise what the lyrics are saying, and that they're taken directly from this passage of the Bible. It's incongruous, I know, and I hope the Lord puts it down to artistic licence, but sometimes in my commercial concerts *Thief in the Night* has to be sandwiched between songs with the tritest and most superficial of lyrics. And it worries me that its message might be overlooked or devalued as a result. Happily, I've been told on more than one occasion that the song has made an impact, and I'm grateful for that encouragement, just as I'm grateful to Paul Field for writing the song.

To my mind, Jesus' second coming has to be the most profound aspect of Christian truth. It's about the hardest to grasp and perhaps, even by some Christians, is taken with the biggest pinch of salt. In fact the teaching is simple — that one day, when the world is complacently believing that all is well, Jesus will return to wind up the old order of things and bring in a new. At that time everyone who is living, and everyone who has ever lived, will stand before Him, some to be personally welcomed into the Lord's family, others to be turned away.

I don't know much more about it than that, and I'm bothered by so many Christian groups who build a whole detailed doctrine and chronology of those last days. I'm certainly not dogmatic about the detail but I'm sure about the principle. Like it or not, there's no getting away from the fact that Jesus' second coming is an integral part of the Bible's message and, because I accept its accuracy about the past on the basis of evidence, and because similarly I accept its accuracy about the present on the grounds of experience, so I accept its reliability about the future on the basis of faith.

In a nutshell, the message of *Thief in the Night* and of this passage is, 'Wake up — it's later than you think!'

SOUND LOGIC

Peter and the other apostles replied: 'We must obey God rather than men!'

When they heard this, they were furious and wanted to put them to death. But a Pharisee named Gamaliel, a teacher of the law, who was honoured by all the people, stood up in the Sanhedrin and ordered that the men be put outside for a little while. Then he addressed them: 'Men of Israel, consider carefully what you intend to do to these men. Some time ago Theudas appeared, claiming to be somebody, and about four hundred men rallied to him. He was killed, all his followers were dispersed, and it all came to nothing. After him, Judas the Galilean appeared in the days of the census and led a band of people in revolt. He too was killed, and all his followers were scattered. Therefore, in the present case I advise you: Leave these men alone! Let them go! For if their purpose or activity is of human origin, it will fail. But if it is from God, you will not be able to stop these men; you will only find yourselves fighting against God.'

His speech persuaded them. They called the apostles in and had them flogged. Then they ordered them not to speak in the name of Jesus, and let them go.

The apostles left the Sanhedrin, rejoicing because they had been counted worthy of suffering disgrace for the Name. Day after day, in the temple courts and from house to house, they never stopped teaching and proclaiming the good news that Jesus is the Christ.

Acts 5: 29, 33-42

It's odd that people should get so flustered and worked up about the Christian faith when they maintain it's all bunkum and make-believe. Why let a fantasy, if that's what it is, get up your nose? It's hardly worth the hassle.

Yet Christianity has always offended and disturbed people. In the early days Christians were thrown to lions, burned as witches, or imprisoned as heretics. Although nowadays there's greater tolerance — at least in the 'free West' — and the worst most of us can expect is harmless mickey-taking or pathetic sarcasm, reactions can still be distinctly prickly or uncomfortable when Christian issues come too close. I can only assume that Jesus and all He stands for presents an unsettling threat to people's cosy life styles.

Gamaliel was a wise old bird. His advice, apart from being wholly logical, was the height of caution. To those who wanted to wipe out all trace of Christianity, together with its followers, in some immediate brutal witch-hunt, he presented the perfect argument. (Could it just be that Jesus was getting through to him?)

Various sects and religious groups, he argued, had come and gone over the years and had made little or no impact. With time, all had burnt themselves out. Probably it would be the same with these Christians. As they scattered, their strength and influence would be diluted until it would disappear altogether. That was assuming of course that the whole thing was man's invention and imagination.

But just suppose these Christians were right, Gamaliel added. Just suppose this Christianity was of God, and that Jesus was who He said He was. 'Not only would we be fighting a losing battle, but we'd be fighting God Himself.' Clearly that was a gamble Gamaliel at least was not prepared to take. Far better, he thought, to watch from the side-lines and do nothing that they might regret later.

Some would say that, after 2,000 years and a remarkable history of achievement and impact, Christianity has stood Gamaliel's test of time.

BRING OUT YOUR FLEECE

Gideon said to God, 'If you will save Israel by my hand as you have promised — look, I will place a wool fleece on the threshing-floor. If there is dew only on the fleece and all the ground is dry, then I will know that you will save Israel by my hand, as you said.' And that is what happened. Gideon rose early the next day; he squeezed the fleece and wrung out the dew — a bowlful of water.

Then Gideon said to God, 'Do not be angry with me. Let me make just one more request. Allow me one more test with the fleece. This time make the fleece dry and the ground covered with dew.' That night God did so. Only the fleece was dry; all the ground was covered with dew.

Judges 6: 36-40

A long time ago this may have been, but human nature doesn't change a bit. Gideon didn't want to make a fool of himself, and neither do we. It wasn't that he disbelieved God's promises of some special and difficult responsibility. It was just that a bit of proof would be nice and reassuring. A sign or a message maybe, or a thunderbolt. Anything that would satisfy that little niggle at the back of the mind that whispered, 'It's all in the imagination.' And so Gideon put out his famous fleece, and twice God gave him the tangible sign he asked for. Twice, notice.

The first time should have been good enough. After all, the odds against a localised shower or a patch of dew on that tiny scale were ludicrous, but Gideon needed a lot of convincing. Maybe it was just a remarkable coincidence. One more time, then he'd believe.

Incredibly, God was patient one more time and the inexplicable happened again. Gideon was convinced and got on with the job.

People today often tell me they'd believe if God gave them a sign. Just a little one — like a 'kerpow!' miracle, or their name blazoned in lights across the sky. Frankly, if God gave them their signs, I doubt if it would make the slightest difference. At least, not for long. You think of all those people who saw Jesus' miracles. A few months afterwards many of them were shouting for His execution.

Some of us, I guess, by our very natures and temperaments genuinely need the occasional practical boost for our faith. Thomas was the classic doubter. 'Unless I see the nail marks in His hands,' he said on hearing news of Jesus' resurrection, 'and put my finger where the nails were, I will not believe.' Lovingly, and without a hint of scolding, Jesus gave Thomas the assurance he needed. At the same time He added, 'Because you have seen me you have believed. Blessed are those who have not seen and yet have believed.'

Maybe there are times when God allows us, and even wants us, to use the 'fleece' principle and test His guidance in some tangible way. I certainly know of Christians who have given God deadlines for some specific action and God has honoured their 'bargaining'. I guess there's a big difference between genuinely wanting to discover God's will with a view to obeying it, and cynically demanding a sign which, if given, we'd probably go to great lengths to explain away.

A RIGHT OLD MOAN

My God, my God, why have you forsaken me?
* Why are you so far from saving me,*
* so far from the words of my groaning?*
O my God, I cry out by day, but you do not answer,
* by night, and am not silent.*

Yet you are enthroned as the Holy One,
* you are the praise of Israel.*
In you our fathers put their trust;
* they trusted and you delivered them.*
They cried to you and were saved;
* in you they trusted and were not disappointed.*

But I am a worm and not a man,
* scorned by men and despised by the people.*
All who see me mock me;
* they hurl insults, shaking their heads:*
'He trusts in the LORD;
* let the LORD rescue him.*
Let him deliver him,
* since he delights in him.'*

Yet you brought me out of the womb;
* you made me trust in you*
* even at my mother's breast.*
From birth I was cast upon you;
* from my mother's womb you have been my God.*
Do not be far from me,
* for trouble is near*
* and there is no-one to help.*

Psalm 22: 1-11

One of the great pressures that living in society puts on us is that we're expected to conform. I've never admitted it before, but I'd quite like to wear an earring — simply because I think they look good. But I know that family, friends and thousands of Christians would pale with dismay, to say the least — and why upset them for something so trivial? (Besides which, I probably haven't the nerve to have my ear pierced!)

The church certainly puts pressure on us to conform as well, and as long as that conformity is to God's Word, then fine. But sometimes the squeeze is on for us to behave or act in ways that square with human, rather than divine, expectations. I'm thinking particularly about the impression that stems from some churches — usually very lively and enthusiastic ones, which in most respects are marvellous — that whenever we approach God it has to be with radiant, happy faces and ecstatic praise. Of course it's fantastic when we can experience that kind of worship but life, even the Christian life, isn't a permanent 'high', and there are times when smiling and singing are the exact opposite of what's in our hearts. The dangerous implication of this always-happy Christianity is that when we're angry or depressed, disappointed or hurt, God is less accessible, or even that we have no business to come to Him in such a mood.

The lesson that the psalm teaches us clearly is that relating to God isn't reserved for the good times. If you read the whole psalm, you'll see that David felt pretty grotty. Sure, God wants our praises and our worship, but equally He wants us to share our grievances. When we're right down in the dumps and when God seems a million miles away, He wants us to tell Him and let Him help shoulder the burden.

The reality of God doesn't change according to our mood and, although He must love it when we can thank and praise Him for all He is and for all He's done, I'm positive that He's just as eager to listen and to bless us when we cry, shout, or just have a right old moan.

JUST IN TIME

There is a time for everything,
and a season for every activity under heaven:
  a time to be born and a time to die,
  a time to plant and a time to uproot,
  a time to kill and a time to heal,
  a time to tear down and a time to build,
  a time to weep and a time to laugh,
  a time to mourn and a time to dance,
  a time to scatter stones and a time to gather them,
  a time to embrace and a time to refrain,
  a time to search and a time to give up,
  a time to keep and a time to throw away,
  a time to tear and a time to mend,
  a time to be silent and a time to speak,
  a time to love and a time to hate,
  a time for war and a time for peace.

Ecclesiastes 3: 1-8

It's amazing how often the telephone will ring at home just as I'm about to sit down to a meal, or someone will knock at the door at the most crucial point in a TV thriller. It's one of those unmentionable laws that seem to conspire to cause maximum frustration!

As a result, our ability to discern the right and appropriate time to take on life's various responsibilities is really quite important. 'There's a time and place for everything,' my mum would tell us as kids, and she was right. The writer of Ecclesiastes said exactly the same thing. (And, in case you wonder why his words are familiar, they're the basis of the old Byrds song *Turn Turn Turn*. OK, so you're too young to remember!)

Often we get into trouble, not because the things we say or do are necessarily wrong, but because our timing is up the spout. Maybe we don't think, perhaps we're too impatient or too lazy. How many people, for instance, regret getting married too early, leaving their education too late, missing a last opportunity to be kind and considerate to an elderly relative? How often we kick ourselves as Christians when the time has been perfect to

make a positive stand for Jesus, and we've chickened out or just been too dozy.

On stage a good sense of timing is vital. In life, too, it's a massive asset.

Maybe these verses will come as a warning as well for the person who's always in a hurry and claims never to have time for anything. 'I'm sorry,' is their stock answer; 'I'd love to but I've no time.' 'What a great idea — but, sorry, no time.' 'Can't talk — sorry, no time.' 'I'd like to help but ...'

Being busy is fine, but what a waste if we're so blinkered and preoccupied that we miss out on something that God has planned for us. Life isn't intended to be one unchanging monotonous experience, but comprises all sorts of emotions, encounters and responsibilities, some of them enjoyable, others not; some rewarding, some painful.

God has given us the time — just enough of it — to do what He wants us to do. It's up to us to find it!

PERCY WHO?

Consider it pure joy, my brothers, whenever you face trials of many kinds, because you know that the testing of your faith develops perseverance. Perseverance must finish its work so that you may be mature and complete, not lacking anything. If any of you lack wisdom, he should ask God, who gives generously to all without finding fault; and it will be given to him. But when he asks, he must believe and not doubt, because he who doubts is like a wave of the sea, blown and tossed by the wind.

Blessed is the man who perseveres under trial, because when he has stood the test, he will receive the crown of life that God has promised to those who love him.

James 1: 2-6, 12

It's a funny word somehow — perseverance. Perhaps because there's less of it around these days, or we've invented more 'hip' equivalents like 'stickability'. At first I thought it meant much the same as patience but, on second thoughts, perseverance is an altogether bigger word. While patience implies quietly and calmly waiting — like me on a Monday night waiting for the Tuesday chart positions to come through (!) — perseverance has a more active quality.

When things are going badly yet you battle on despite the setbacks, that's perseverance. When the odds seem stacked against you and the faint hearts round about are giving up, then perseverance is having the guts to get stuck in and keep going.

I know she won't mind my using her as an example, but my friend Sue Barker has a whole load of it when it comes to tennis and, if I wore one, I'd take my hat off to her! For the past few years Sue has been having real problems with her game. First it was a back injury, then a service difficulty, then a muscle strain, then a timing problem, and so on and so on. Inevitably friends and players were telling her, 'It's time to hang up your racquet and retire,' but Sue was convinced she had it in her to win. So she went on playing, determined to claw her way back up the tennis ratings. Whether she succeeds is irrelevant, but, if perseverance is anything to go by, she certainly should!

Now, apply it to living the Christian life and you'll realise that, just like Paul, James is under no delusion about Christianity being an easy escapist jolly sing-along. There *will* be trials, difficulty and hardship. We *will* be discouraged, disappointed; we may even be depressed at times. Our feelings may get hurt, and we'll surely be tired, and we either give up and go with the crowd, or we persevere and stick with Jesus.

'Blessed', says James, 'is the man who perseveres...'

ALL AT SEA

During the fourth watch of the night Jesus went out to them, walking on the lake.

'Lord, if it's you,' Peter replied, 'tell me to come to you on the water.'

'Come,' he said.

Then Peter got down out of the boat and walked on the water to Jesus. But when he saw the wind, he was afraid and, beginning to sink, cried out, 'Lord, save me!'

Immediately Jesus reached out his hand and caught him. 'You of little faith,' he said, 'why did you doubt?'

And when they climbed into the boat, the wind died down. Then those who were in the boat worshipped him, saying, 'Truly you are the Son of God.'
Matthew 14: 25, 28-33

'How can you believe in God when the world's likely to be blown to pieces tomorrow or the day after?' That was a question lobbed at me by one fifteen-year-old, and I guess it reflects the fear and uncertainty of millions of kids growing up under the threat of nuclear war.

Obviously there's nothing in the Bible that refers directly to nuclear warheads, missile bases, unilateral disarmament, and all the other jargon that's become part of our lives. But, like so many issues, there is absolutely clear teaching about a principle. In this case, the key question is, 'Who's in control?'

I tell you, if I believed our eternal destiny was in the hands of world leaders and politicians, I'd pack it in now and emigrate to the farthest desert island. I have no great 'ring of confidence' when it comes to the so-called major powers. But my confidence doesn't have to be in people like you and me, who are just as vulnerable and likely to panic at the first sign of aggro. Despite what we're led to believe, they are not the power ultimately in charge. God is greater than the guys that press the buttons and no way has He abandoned His world to the maniacs. God is still in control and loves what He's created.

Can you imagine what a relief it was for Peter when he discovered that Jesus was in control, even of the waves and the natural laws? Suddenly there was no need to be afraid, because Jesus knew the problem and He could cope. Peter was safe.

I don't know exactly how the world will end, or even if one day there may be a nuclear war. But it's because I know that there is a God that I'm neither afraid nor depressed by the prospect. That doesn't mean to say I'm not concerned and I have respect for many Christians who feel it's right to campaign and protest about the build-up of weapons.

But Jesus says, 'Don't be afraid,' — and like Peter, who got more than his socks wet, I have reason to believe Him!

MORE BORING TELEVISION!

Go to the ant, you sluggard;
  consider its ways and be wise!
It has no commander,
  no overseer or ruler,
yet it stores its provisions in summer
  and gathers its food at harvest.
How long will you lie there, you sluggard?
  When will you get up from your sleep?
A little sleep, a little slumber,
  a little folding of the hands to rest —
and poverty will come on you like a bandit
  and scarcity like an armed man.

Proverbs 6: 6-11

I can't believe that Christians should ever find life boring. I know some do but, at the risk of being shot down, I suspect the fault is one hundred per cent theirs. Doing nothing is boring. We get bored when we overdose on television. Boredom, to be blunt, is born of mental or physical laziness — or probably both.

'Sluggard' is an old-fashioned word, meaning someone who's lazy, and it's a pretty offensive description. Maybe it's a word we should restore to our vocabulary, but it's frightening how many people you meet who are reluctant to make any effort of any kind in any direction. At work, at home, in relationships, and even in the church, they want to settle for the least they can get away with. So the order of the day is maximum return for minimum effort. That's a horribly destructive philosophy, and it certainly doesn't square with Christianity.

The writer of these wise old proverbs was obviously a lover of nature, and draws on all manner of insect and animal life for his illustrations. Take a lesson from the ant, he says, always busy, always frantically fetching and carrying. True. When did you last spot an ant asleep or taking it easy?

Like so many things of course, we need to keep a proper balance. Our minds and bodies need the right amount of rest and relaxation. On the rare evening off, I love to sit in front of the telly with an Indian take-away, and do absolutely nothing. It's the same on holiday. I must be one of the most dreary people to go away with, because I do little besides lie in the sun and listen to music — but I need that time to unwind and recharge the batteries. The rest of my year is full, active and demanding, and that ideally is the way it should, and I suspect could, be for everyone.

When there's so much need and opportunity on our doorsteps, there's something radically wrong with a bored Christian, and a hefty kick in the pants is required for a lazy one. As I say, the chances are that they're one and the same.

ONLY HUMAN

Listen to my prayer, O God,
  do not ignore my plea;
  hear me and answer me.

If an enemy were insulting me,
  I could endure it;
if a foe were raising himself against me,
  I could hide from him.
But it is you, a man like myself,
  my companion, my close friend,
with whom I once enjoyed sweet fellowship
  as we walked with the throng at the house of God.

Cast your cares on the LORD
  and he will sustain you;
  he will never let the righteous fall.

Psalm 55: 1, 2a, 12-14, 22

One of the hardest knocks to take in life is being let down and betrayed by people we trust. Maybe a friend who we've known for years starts whispering and criticising behind our back. One act of disloyalty may destroy years of unquestioning confidence between man and wife. The bottom can suddenly drop from a youngster's world when mum or dad ignores a promise; and mum and dad can be equally devastated when their children return love with resentment and spite.

Disappointments from colleagues and acquaintances — we can live with those. Disappointment from those we love and think we know so well can be emotionally crippling.

David had such an experience. That friend who he'd loved and respected was suddenly like a different man. It was hard to believe how much he'd changed. They'd had such good times together, joking, discussing, and relying on each other. Now it was as though that bond between them had never existed. Every ounce of trust had vanished.

David was distraught and angry and he told God so. His conversations with God weren't reserved for 'religious' moods, but he'd learned to share his frustration and despondencies too. And David found that helpful. The burden was easier to bear when part of it at least was offloaded on the Lord.

Nevertheless, I'm sure that the pain went on. As far as I know, there's no quick or easy remedy for emotional wounds, and David never suggested that the hurting stopped, only that he was given strength to cope with it.

If you think your pain is more dreadful than most, just remember that Jesus was betrayed too, for a handful of coins. He knows what it's like, and that at least is a comfort.

But maybe comfort's not enough. Let me quote a reaction from someone who read my original manuscript, which ended at the last paragraph. I feel it gives a fuller perspective. 'Eighteen months ago,' she said, 'I'd have gone along with the idea that the hurting goes on and that we're merely given strength to cope with it. But having personally experienced an amazing release from long-standing and very deep hurts, I'm now convinced that God not only understands but He can also do something about it. Remember that Isaiah says God "binds up the broken-hearted".'

I stand corrected!

BUT WHY JESUS?

He is the image of the invisible God, the firstborn over all creation. For by him all things were created: things in heaven and on earth, visible and invisible, whether thrones or powers or rulers or authorities; all things were created by him and for him. He is before all things, and in him all things hold together. And he is the head of the body, the church; he is the beginning and the firstborn among the dead, so that in everything he might have the supremacy. For God was pleased to have all his fulness dwell in him, and through him to reconcile to himself all things, whether things on earth or things in heaven, by making peace through his blood, shed on the cross.

Colossians 1: 15-20

You may need to read these verses through a few times before you get the gist. It's heavy stuff, I know, and I certainly don't pretend to grasp it fully, but it's here because we can't be reminded too often of exactly who Jesus is, and this little passage spells it out, perhaps more clearly, powerfully and magnificently than anywhere else in the Bible.

The claim is that Jesus not only shows us God, but He actually has God's nature and therefore is God. Also, Jesus is supreme over all else, and somehow in Him are all the secrets and mysteries of our universe.

As I say, they're mind-expanding concepts, but it's so vital that we know who it is we follow. For many of us, our only impression of Jesus comes from stage or screen portrayals and, inevitably, they're wildly lopsided. Jesus is far more than a gifted founder of a religion, for instance. There are scores of men like that scattered through history; some have left their mark, others are long forgotten. To think of Jesus merely as an example or an ideal to try to copy is to sell Him so far short that it borders on the insulting. Even to regard Him as 'our buddy', who's useful to have around when times are tough, can so easily reduce our respect and rob Jesus of His rightful authority and majesty.

It's a silly understatement, but these verses remind me that Jesus is important and that He wants and deserves every ounce of worship and obedience and love I can give Him. When I went to Buckingham Palace to receive my OBE from the Queen, everyone, quite rightly, showed tremendous deference towards her. Some of us in the line-up had to bow, others were to kneel. There was a strict code of conduct and etiquette, and no one would have dreamed of breaching it. This, after all, was the monarch.

Yet here in Paul's letter we're told that it was by Jesus that thrones, powers, rulers and authorities were created in the first place, and that it's Jesus who has the ultimate power and who has ultimate control.

My personal preference is for church worship that's warm and relaxed and where God is made approachable. Just occasionally it does me good to visit a church, or a cathedral maybe, where the beauty and the grandeur and the solemnity help me to sharpen focus on Jesus. I'm reminded then that, although I know Him best as a loving friend and Saviour, He is also awesome and all-powerful God. It's good to keep the balance.

DON'T BLAME GOD

When tempted, no-one should say,
'God is tempting me.' For God cannot
be tempted by evil, nor does he tempt
anyone; but each one is tempted when,
by his own evil desire, he is dragged
away and enticed. Then, after desire
has conceived, it gives birth to sin; and
sin when it is full-grown, gives birth to
death.

James 1: 13-15

Satan gets off very lightly, it seems to me, when it comes to our apportioning of blame. When things go wrong, we have a go at God, at social conditions, at family relationships, anything but the root evil which is the Devil himself.

The whole subject of evil in all its sad and many forms — suffering, violence, poverty, hatred, oppression and so on — is so hard to come to terms with, and sometimes Christians tend to be insensitive, over-quick and naïve in their explaining and condemning.

But, while it's foolish to oversimplify and dangerous to set ourselves up as judges of others, we can be sure that responsible for all that spoils and degrades our world is not God, but God's enemy. It makes a heck of a difference to know who we're fighting. It's only when we recognise the enemy that we can plan our war more effectively and at least focus our attack and resistance in the right direction.

I reckon a lot of us feel miserable as we fret and struggle to overcome some problem in our lives, and all the time we're fighting the wrong enemy. Maybe we pit our will power or our self-control against some recurring temptation or habit and find it's a one-sided battle. Will power and self-control don't stand a chance, and that's depressing and demoralising. But identify the Devil as the source of the problem and mobilise God's resources against him, and it's a different story. This time it's Satan who's on the losing side and who will get the eventual knock-out blow.

If only we recognised the reality of that spiritual conflict, I'm sure we'd be more successful at dealing not only with personal hassles but with national and international ones too. So much energy, time and protest is directed to symptoms of evil, instead of understanding and tackling the cause of it!

So back to James — and it's hard to quarrel with the truth of his unhappy sequence — first the thought from the evil source, then the dragging away (maybe there's not always much of a struggle!), then, when the thought becomes a deed, temptation turns to sin, and eventually unforgiven sin results in death and permanent separation from God. Mercifully it isn't an inevitable progression.

DARE TO BE DIFFERENT

Therefore, I urge you, brothers, in view of God's mercy, to offer your bodies as living sacrifices, holy and pleasing to God — which is your spiritual worship. Do not conform any longer to the pattern of this world, but be transformed by the renewing of your mind. Then you will be able to test and approve what God's will is — his good, pleasing and perfect will.

Romans 12: 1-2

'Cloning' seems to have become an 'in' word over recent years. As I understand it, a clone is an exact replica of someone else, someone so similar that it's impossible to spot the difference. 'Conforming', the word that Paul uses, isn't quite that extreme, but the idea of fitting into a pattern has a similar ring. Instinctively, to some degree, we all do it. We don't like to be conspicuous or 'peculiar'. It's easier, more comfortable, to blend in with our surroundings, and so we try to behave the same, look the same, and live the same. We're embarrassed, or even a bit afraid, to stand out as different.

What a pressure that is against practical Christian conduct. Deep down a distinct tweak of conscience tells us there's something in Christianity that's good and worth exploring but, no sooner than the urge is on us, it's overtaken by fear of public reaction. 'She's gone religious.' 'What a hypocrite!' 'It won't last.' 'He's dropped out of his tree.' You know the sort of thing.

More often than not, the life style expected by the society we live in is more important to us than the life style demanded by God. And, because society sniggers and laughs at us behind our backs if we're 'out of line', it's easier and more comfortable to shuffle back!

God needs people who'll dare to be different. Boys and girls, for instance, who won't get involved with smoking or drugs just because their friends are hooked. Men and women who'll resist the pressure for lives and resources to be governed by 'keeping up with the Joneses'. People of strength and integrity whose priorities and values can't be threatened or undermined by the world's topsy-turvy standards.

Here's a back-to-front example of what I mean. A while ago I visited a very respectable Anglican church in a posh area of Surrey. It was a small congregation but there, in the middle of them, sat a young guy with the most exotic pink and green cockatoo hairstyle you've ever seen. I shouldn't have been surprised, but I was — even more maybe when he got up and went forward for Communion. When I'd recovered from the shock, I felt real pleasure and respect for that guy. The pleasure was for a vivid reminder of the freedom that the Lord gives us to be ourselves in His family — and there's nothing in the Bible that prohibits colourful hairstyles! The respect was for someone who had the guts to be different when the pressure would have been to conform and look 'respectable'.

Someone said that it's easy to pray in a dormitory full of bishops, but not so easy in an army barrack-room. God doesn't want Christian chameleons who'll conveniently adopt the look of their surroundings. On the contrary, He requires us to be gloriously different

THIRST QUENCHER

When a Samaritan woman came to draw water, Jesus said to her, 'Will you give me a drink?' (His disciples had gone into the town to buy food.)

The Samaritan woman said to him, 'You are a Jew and I am a Samaritan woman. How can you ask me for a drink?' (For Jews do not associate with Samaritans.)

Jesus answered her, 'If you knew the gift of God and who it is that asks you for a drink, you would have asked him and he would have given you living water.'

'Sir,' the woman said, 'you have nothing to draw with and the well is deep. Where can you get this living water? Are you greater than our father Jacob, who gave us the well and drank from it himself, as did also his sons and flocks and herds?'

Jesus answered, 'Everyone who drinks this water will be thirsty again, but whoever drinks the water I give him will never thirst. Indeed, the water I give him will become in him a spring of water welling up to eternal life.'

The woman said to him, 'Sir, give me this water so that I won't get thirsty and have to keep coming here to draw water.'

John 4: 7-15

Despite all the facades and pretence and smoke-screens that people put up when it comes to religion, I'm positive that most of us have a deep longing to find real and satisfying answers to life's question-marks. Our sport and hobbies, our work, and even our relationships, can be fulfilling up to a point, but none of them are guaranteed permanent. Any one can let us down at any time and, even if we strike lucky and find all-round success, there's still the niggle that there might be more.

I remember feeling that way so well, soon after my career was under way. There was that incredible 'high' on stage with the Shadows for an hour or so, with girls shrieking and screaming, and then back to the hotel and anticlimax. The big let-down. Was this really the extent of it? We were famous, popular and rich, and yet it didn't satisfy. There had to be more. Some time later Mick Jagger was publicly sharing the same frustration: 'I can't get no satisfaction'.

The problem is that we look for that elusive fulfilment in the wrong places. We reckon it comes from a secure income, active sex-life, or competitive 'success'. So that's where we direct our energies and attention — only to be frustrated and disillusioned when our appetites are left wanting more.

The woman at the well was a classic example. If you dig out your Bible and follow the story through, you'll see that, behind the respectable and self-sufficient impression, was a life that was morally bankrupt. But she wouldn't admit it, at least not at first, and perhaps didn't even recognise it.

Her first thoughts were to fill the buckets and, if Jesus was in the business of improved water supply, then He was worth chatting up! Gradually the light dawned, and she realised that, instead of helping her with her pails, which would be empty again by tomorrow, Jesus was offering to fill and satisfy her empty life.

There's a lovely invitation at the beginning of Isaiah, chapter 55: 'Come, all you who are thirsty,' it says, 'come to the waters; and you who have no money, come, buy and eat! Come, buy wine and milk without money and without cost'.

If you know you have a thirst, why swig salt water? It tastes rotten and makes you even thirstier. But Jesus' fountain satisfies permanently and tastes a darn sight better!

WHY ME?

Now I want to know, brothers, that what has happened to me has really served to advance the gospel. As a result, it has become clear throughout the whole palace guard and to everyone else that I am in chains for Christ. Because of my chains, most of the brothers in the Lord have been encouraged to speak the word of God more courageously and fearlessly.

The important thing is that in every way, whether from false motives or true, Christ is preached. And because of this I rejoice.
                    Philippians 1: 12-14, 18b

Now this isn't the complete answer, by any means, to that perplexing problem of why God allows hardship and suffering. But at least it sheds a ray of light.

I can just imagine Paul's friends and relatives being totally bewildered and dismayed when they heard the news that Jesus' great and fearless ambassador had been thrown into a dingy Roman jail. What had Paul done to deserve it? Surely he'd been doing a marvellous job for God? Why had He allowed a tragedy like this? Familiar questions, I'm sure, that inevitably pass through our minds when we hear of accidents, illnesses or tragedies that befall people who just don't seem to deserve it. It's all so unfair and such a waste — or so it seems.

Well, obviously Paul didn't think his imprisonment was a waste. True, he could have been out and about preaching the Word in other parts of the world and, from our perspective, that might have been better. But God's strategy was different and, from what appears to be a major setback for Paul's cause, there were unexpected compensations. Paul recognises them and, far from feeling sorry for himself, locked up and on prison rations, he could tell the Christians at Philippi that he was actually rejoicing!

Look what was happening. Not only were the prison guards and

authorities challenged by Paul's practical witness under dreadful circumstances, but Christians round about were spurred on to be more courageous and outspoken. Far from proving a setback to the gospel, Paul's prison sentence was being used by God to actually advance it; from an apparent disaster, great things were resulting.

Now I know it isn't always easy to discern that happening. Sometimes there's a tragic and inexplicable event and, try as we might, it's impossible to detect anything positive. On other occasions, God's hand is more obvious, and I think immediately of David Watson's death from cancer as an example. On the one hand, I know that I and probably many others of his friends wondered why such an outstanding preacher and man of God should have his ministry ended so abruptly. Yet, with hindsight, everyone recognises that David's courage and absolute trust in God's love and goodness right through his illness to the time of his death were and will continue to be the most fantastic comfort and reassurance to countless hundreds of people.

Rather than agonise over why God permits any particular circumstance, it might be more profitable for us to pray that God will give us just a fraction of the faith and courage of Paul or David if something similar ever happened to us.

NOTHING TO PAY

With what shall I come before the LORD
  and bow down before the exalted God?
Shall I come before him with burnt offerings,
  with calves a year old?
Will the LORD be pleased with thousands of rams,
  with ten thousand rivers of oil?
Shall I offer my firstborn for my transgression,
  the fruit of my body for the sin of my soul?
He has showed you, O man, what is good.
  And what does the LORD require of you?
To act justly and to love mercy
  and to walk humbly with your God.

Micah 6: 6-8

'I love God so much,' a lady called Dorothy wrote to me recently, 'and I long to repay Him, but I feel such a failure for God. I hope I'm not, but I search my life and realise that I give Him nothing.'

Since then I'd like to think that Dorothy may have come across these verses from Micah, although it's a book that's easily missed without systematic Bible study. We mustn't get hung up on this idea of needing to repay God for what He's done for us. The debt we owe would be so colossal that any hopes of repayment are as likely as our scaling Everest. I could never repay God for what He's given me in terms of spiritual life now and in the future. And neither could you. Mercifully, He doesn't require repayment, or even suggest that there's any outstanding debt. What God gave to you and me in Jesus is a free gift, and we have to accept it gladly and gratefully as that. Gifts given with love have no repayment terms attached.

In Old Testament times, of course, God's people had no Jesus to be grateful for, and they believed that the bigger and better their offerings the more likely they were to impress and please Him. A calf maybe, or a whole herd of goats. What about an oil-field or, in desperation, even a youngest child? What a hopeless and awful prospect if that's how it had to be. But it isn't, and Dorothy and others, whose enjoyment of God is spoilt because they think they owe Him all the time, need to take Micah's reminder to heart.

Putting our life savings in the collection plate, ten years of missionary service in Bangladesh, even a lifetime on the church council, are empty and meaningless unless they're the expression of a heart that loves Him and loves other people.

Years after Micah, Jesus was asked to pinpoint the greatest Commandment. Remember the answer? 'Love the Lord your God with all your heart and with all your soul and with all your mind and with all your strength. The second is this — love your neighbour as yourself.'

Stop fretting then about debts and repayments. There are none. God and His world just ask for a lot of loving!

ONE HUMP OR TWO . . .?

'Woe to you, teachers of the law and Pharisees, you hypocrites! You give a tenth of your spices — mint, dill and cummin. But you have neglected the more important matters of the law — justice, mercy and faithfulness. You should have practised the latter, without neglecting the former. You blind guides! You strain out a gnat but swallow a camel.

'Woe to you, teachers of the law and Pharisees, you hypocrites! You are like whitewashed tombs, which look beautiful on the outside but on the inside are full of dead men's bones and everything unclean. In the same way, on the outside you appear to people as righteous but on the inside you are full of hypocrisy and wickedness.'

Matthew 23: 23, 24, 27, 28

You can't say Jesus didn't have a sense of humour — although the Pharisees, I imagine, were about as funny as a wet bank holiday — and, even in the midst of a really scathing attack on this hypocritical bunch of religious leaders, He must have had a twinkle in His eye at the thought of swallowing a camel. I bet He'd have loved *The Goon Show!*

We should never take ourselves so seriously that we stifle our sense of humour. To be able to laugh at ourselves occasionally, and even at some of the things we do and say in the name of Christianity, is healthy and harmless. When we lose that ability, there's a danger of becoming over-intense, somewhat unattractive, and a wee bit disturbing. Remember that all good things come from God, and that includes laughter — from a titter to a state of helpless falling about. That's why I loved the show *Godspell* so much. It probably didn't challenge many to think through any deep spiritual issues, but it caused hundreds of folk to discover that the face of Christianity isn't always stern and severe. I'm sure that was first a shock, and then a pleasant surprise!

However, just as there's a time for a joke, so there's a time to be serious, and certainly Jesus' criticism of the Pharisees was no laughing matter. On the face of it, the highly-regarded Pharisees were models of religious virtue. It would seem in fact they were rather nasty people. Nowhere in the Bible does Jesus speak so fiercely and with such round condemnation. There's no trace here of the gentle compassion He showed to the prostitute and the tax-man. They knew they were sinners and deserved to be punished. Instead they were restored and forgiven. The Pharisees believed they were righteous and deserved praise. What they got was a firm kick up the ... what they got was a firm kick!

Be quite clear about it. Going through the motions of being religious may impress friends and family, but with God it means nothing. Mouthing religious words and doing pious things is a worse than useless charade unless our attitudes and motives are right first. Before you apply all this to other people, examine first whether you're the one who's getting all hot and bothered about trivial gnats when there's half a camel down your throat!

NO IMMUNITY

But we have this treasure in jars of clay to show that this all-surpassing power is from God and not from us. We are hard pressed on every side, but not crushed; perplexed, but not in despair; persecuted, but not abandoned; struck down, but not destroyed.

Therefore we do not lose heart. Though outwardly we are wasting away, yet inwardly we are being renewed day by day. For our light and momentary troubles are achieving for us an eternal glory that far outweighs them all. So we fix our eyes not on what is seen, but on what is unseen. For what is seen is temporary, but what is unseen is eternal.

2 Corinthians 4:7-9, 16-18

There's a fast-growing wing of the church that seems to teach that, once you're a Christian, you can rightfully claim some sort of immunity from life's pressures and calamities. The gist of it, as far as I can make out, is that God wants the very best for His people and so illnesses, depressions or 'ill fortune' can only be the result of our lack of faith or failure to claim God's victory.

Now personally I have a lot of trouble with that kind of emphasis because, although I certainly believe that the Lord has great things in store for us in eternity, I also reckon He keeps us in the real world, where we're still vulnerable to its pain and hardships.

I can't believe, for instance, that an influenza bug is any respecter of persons and it's just as likely to zap a Christian working in a crowded office as the militant atheist at the next desk.

The difference is that the Christian is promised the grace to cope with the problems and discomforts and to come through them with faith intact.

Surely that was Paul's experience. He was blitzed with all manner of pain and hardships and, reading between the lines of his letter to Corinth, he was feeling pretty out of sorts. In the next chapter he talks about 'groaning' and longing 'to be clothed with our heavenly dwelling'.

The point is that, despite the setbacks and the burdens, Paul was never disillusioned or disappointed with Jesus. Outwardly things could be falling apart, the enemy often seemed to have the upper hand, and physically he was getting weaker and more tired. Life itself was as brittle and as susceptible to cracks and damage as a clay jar but, whatever the earthly setbacks, Paul knew they were temporary and trivial. His sights were fixed on what was beyond, and that outweighed every headache, every jail sentence, and every human sadness put together.

A BAD PATCH

Save me, O God,
* for the waters have come up to my neck.*
I sink in the miry depths,
* where there is no foothold.*
I have come into the deep waters;
* the floods engulf me.*
I am worn out calling for help;
* my throat is parched.*
My eyes fail,
* looking for my God.*

But I pray to you, O LORD,
* in the time of your favour;*
in your great love, O God,
* answer me with your sure salvation.*
Rescue me from the mire,
* do not let me sink;*
deliver me from those who hate me,
* from the deep waters.*
Do not let the floodwaters engulf me
* or the depths swallow me up*
* or the pit close its mouth over me.*
Answer me, O LORD, out of the goodness of your love;
* in your great mercy turn to me.*
Do not hide your face from your servant;
* answer me quickly, for I am in trouble.*

Psalm 69: 1-3, 13-17

I wonder how honest we Christians are with each other. If we stripped away all the pretence and spiritual image-building that goes on, I think we'd be amazed and probably weep with relief to find just how normal and commonplace our 'secret' moods and anxieties are.

I have come to be slightly wary of those super-spiritual brothers and sisters who always seem to be experiencing life's 'ups' and know nothing of its 'downs'. Every day they're on top of the world, happily praising the Lord and enjoying marvellous fellowship. Miracles and dramatic answers to prayer seem almost a daily occurrence.

Now perhaps that's how it ought to be. In fact I'm sure it should, and I don't mean to be cynical. Nevertheless I suspect the great majority of us can relate more easily to David, who knew as much about the spiritual troughs as the mountain-tops.

It's hard to believe that this anguished cry for help was written by the same guy who, in Psalm 23, was basking in the assurance of a God who was a loving, caring shepherd. Psalm 121 is over the moon about God never sleeping or being off-duty, and other psalms bubble over with confidence, gratitude and devotion. But not this one. Psalm 69 reveals a desperate man, who despairs over prayers that are unanswered and a God who seems remote and inaccessible. One problem is heaped up on another and, whichever way he turns, there seems no solution.

So what's gone wrong? Had God deserted David in a crisis? Or did David's faith suddenly dry up? Neither! Before you jump in the lake with depression, read on to the end of the psalm. The good news is that David comes through it, and I reckon it was because he kept his *mind* fixed on what he knew to be true. Although he was 'worn out' with praying and although he had eye-strain trying to discover God's guidance, it never occurred to him to give up or to doubt that God still cared. He may not have understood why there were no apparent answers to all his pleading but he never wavered from the conviction that the Lord was in control. He didn't understand. he was tired, depressed and desperately worried. Emotionally he felt ghastly. But David's faith was based not on how he felt but on what he knew.

So he could pray, '... in your great love, O God, answer me with your sure salvation'. And, in His time, God did of course.

QUICK OFF THE MARK

This man had gone to Jerusalem to worship, and on his way home was sitting in his chariot reading the book of Isaiah the prophet. The Spirit told Philip, 'Go to that chariot and stay near it.'

Then Philip ran up to the chariot and heard the man reading Isaiah the prophet. 'Do you understand what you are reading?' Philip asked.

'How can I,' he said, 'unless someone explains it to me?' So he invited Philip to come up and sit with him.

The eunuch asked Philip, 'Tell me, please, who is the prophet talking about, himself or someone else?' Then Philip began with that very passage of Scripture and told him the good news about Jesus.

Acts 8:27b-31, 34, 35

Don't be surprised, if you're a Christian, to find yourself in situations where people ask for your help or advice. It's natural to think that conversations like the one Philip had are best left to the experts, or at least to more experienced Christians who know what they're talking about. But that's not always true. Philip was the only Christian around at that time and, if he'd clammed up, the Ethiopian would have gone on his way and perhaps would never again have been so open and interested. As it was, Philip grabbed the opportunity, launched in, and spoke up, and the guy was converted.

How would you cope in a modern-day parallel situation? There you are, travelling in a railway carriage, with someone who's reading a Bible. Before you know it, you're in conversation and your fellow-traveller is asking important and genuine questions about Christianity. Would you have any answers? Would you be able to direct him to parts of the Bible that were relevant? Would you have the courage to do as Philip did and tell him 'the good news about Jesus'?

You might be nervous and feel dreadfully inadequate, but all of us should be prepared and ready to tackle an opportunity like that if it arises.

And don't kid yourself that it's wildly improbable. In my experience more and more people are wanting to know what makes Christians tick and are asking serious searching questions about God and whether it's really possible to know Him. Maybe you'll be the only Christian they ever meet and if *you* don't share the good news then no one will.

'Always be ready,' wrote Paul, 'to give a reason for the hope that is in you.' And he was writing to run-of-the-mill Christians, not just to an elite bunch of scholars or speakers.

If your reaction is, 'No, I couldn't,' let me suggest three reasons why I think you could. Firstly, as a Christian, you have an experience to share. You know what Jesus has done for you, and no one can dispute an experience. Secondly, there are books and cassette tapes and Bible college courses to help you discover more about the Bible. OK, so it's a mental effort but, if it's a responsibility you need to take seriously, what kind of an excuse is that? And, thirdly, there's God's promise to give you the grace and ability to share Jesus in a way you could never do with just your own resources.

So it isn't a matter of *could* you be a Philip. The answer is yes, you could. The real issue is *would* you, if the opportunity arose?

TWO LOVES

Dear friends, let us love one another, for love comes from God. Everyone who loves has been born of God and knows God. Whoever does not love does not know God, because God is love. This is how God showed his love among us: He sent his one and only Son into the world that we might live through him. This is love, not that we loved God, but that he loved us and sent his Son as an atoning sacrifice for our sins. Dear friends, since God so loved us, we also ought to love one another.

There is no fear in love. But perfect love drives out fear, because fear has to do with punishment. The man who fears is not made perfect in love.

We love because he first loved us. If anyone says, 'I love God,' yet hates his brother, he is a liar. For anyone who does not love his brother, whom he has seen, cannot love God, whom he has not seen. And he has given us this command: Whoever loves God must also love his brother.

1 John 4:7-11, 18-21

When you think of it, it's almost a cheek to try and add to, explain, or even comment on some of these Bible extracts, because they're so totally self-sufficient. You don't need me or anyone else to help you understand.

Perhaps all I can offer is an apology. An apology for contributing in countless song lyrics to the idea that love is merely a slushy fragile emotion which we fall into and out of at the drop of a hat, and over which we have virtually no control.

Sadly, the word has been so misused and devalued that we may need to check back on the most comprehensive definition of love ever written, in 1 Corinthians, chapter 13. If you have a Bible, check it out and apply it to these few verses from John's famous chapter.

You'll discover that God's love for us isn't fickle or brittle, liable to evaporate at the slightest hint of unfaithfulness on our part. In fact it isn't dependent on our response at all. God's love is unconditional, totally reliable, and actively caring. Whether we want it, receive it, or even acknowledge it is beside the point. The reality is that it exists for each one of us individually.

And for us Christians it's that very same quality of love that we have to demonstrate to one another. We have to love, even though we're not necessarily loved in return. Our love must be constant and dependable. Our love isn't about sentiment and platitudes, but is compassionate and practical, and gets involved and makes sacrifices and receives knocks.

If we say we love God, writes John, we are liars if we don't reflect at least a glimmer of divine concern for those around us.

I don't know about you, but that stops me very short in my tracks.

HAND ME DOWN

But as for you, continue in what you have learned and have become convinced of, because you know those from whom you learned it, and how from infancy you have known the holy Scriptures, which are able to make you wise for salvation through faith in Christ Jesus. All Scripture is God-breathed and is useful for teaching, rebuking, correcting and training in righteousness, so that the man of God may be thoroughly equipped for every good work.

2 Timothy 3:14-17

I'm sure it is true that most of us get our Christian teaching and encouragement from older Christians. I don't mean older in years necessarily, but older in the faith. I know, when I was asking all my questions over twenty years ago, there were just two or three guys around my age who had been Christians for some time, who were sure of what they believed, and were willing to patiently share it with me. They in turn had been taught and encouraged by an old Bible class leader no longer with us. He would have had no idea about the future ripple effect of his faithful and unspectacular work.

In this instance Paul is the teacher and Timothy the new young Christian. The advice is what every newcomer to Christianity over the centuries needs to get clearly fixed in his mind. Firstly, he is encouraged to *go on* learning, and what sound wisdom that is. There is never any point when we can sit back as Christians and say we know it all, and the fact that we read through St John's Gospel two years ago doesn't mean that we have exhausted its meaning. The greatest Bible scholars are likely to say that they are still wearing L-plates when it comes to understanding all that is in the Bible and, because it is a book that 'lives' and is relevant to every changing mood and situation, what we get out of it today may be quite different to how God will use it tomorrow.

Secondly then, realise that the Bible is no ordinary textbook. What is it that makes it the world's permanent bestseller? Why is it an automatic assumption that every castaway will want it on a desert island? How come it goes on giving such comfort and hope to millions of people, no matter how extreme their hardship or suffering? Paul reminds Timothy of the answer; because it is 'God-breathed'. Far from a tedious old relic about strange kings and remote preachers, it is a book which somehow has the ability to speak directly into our situation, whatever it might be.

Maybe it is encouragement we need, or comfort, maybe direction, or even a rap on the knuckles. Maybe we're desperate for hope and reassurance, or simply a reason for living. Whatever our mood or condition or personality, God uses His Word, the Bible, to go right to the heart of the matter and to show us what is true.

Read it — or, better still, have a daily soak in it — and you'll be equipped for the business of real living.

GOOD OVER EVIL

As he went along, he saw a man blind from birth. His disciples asked him, 'Rabbi, who sinned, this man or his parents, that he was born blind?'

'Neither this man nor his parents sinned,' said Jesus, 'but this happened so that the work of God might be displayed in his life. As long as it is day, we must do the work of him who sent me. Night is coming, when no-one can work. While I am in the world, I am the light of the world.'

Having said this, he spat on the ground, made some mud with the saliva, and put it on the man's eyes. 'Go,' he told him, 'wash in the pool of Siloam' (this word means Sent). So the man went and washed, and came home seeing.

John 9: 1-7

Usually as far as sin is concerned, we're the masters of disguise. No-one knows and no-one can tell. Except, that is, when it leaves those telltale marks on the body — too much alcohol, for instance, rots the liver. Over-eating or gluttony can accelerate heart disease, quite apart from the dreaded flab. Free and easy sex may result in VD, and mental strain and even breakdown can be the consequence of lying and deceit.

What you sow, says the old proverb, is what you reap, and that's a sound Biblical principle — up to a point. For, while it's true that sin sometimes causes physical damage, it's most certainly not true that physical damage is necessarily the result of sin. It's a cruel old wives' tale and a terrible distortion of God's love that suggests that an illness or accident is necessarily God's punishment for wickedness.

Now I don't know why good and innocent people seem so often to be the ones struck down by some awful affliction. I've no answer to explain why thousands might be injured or wiped out by a sudden natural disaster. All I *am* positive of is that the God I've discovered in the Bible and through Jesus is concerned to forgive and heal, not to hurt and maim.

'What have I done to deserve this?' is almost a stock response to sudden tragedy. The chances are that the answer is 'nothing at all'. How dare anyone imply that there's personal blame attached to the cancer victim or to the innocent party in a road crash? And what of the mentally retarded child or the baby born blind? The disciples' assumption about the blind man and his parents was unthinkable. Of course no one was at fault; Jesus firmly put paid to the idea. Far from any hurtful accusation, He turned their negative assumption to a positive possibility. Through the man's healing, people would see evidence of God's power at work, and good would come from what was bad.

Perhaps that's the question we should be asking. Not who's to blame, or was it deserved, but what good can result? Sometimes it's amazing how God's grace and strength can radiate from sick, frail people. And the impact they can have on others is more telling than many an eloquent sermon.

NO CHOICE

'Why have we fasted,' they say,
'and you have not seen it?
Why have we humbled ourselves,
and you have not noticed?'
'Yet on the day of your fasting, you do
as you please
and exploit all your workers.
Your fasting ends in quarrelling and
strife,
and in striking each other with
wicked fists.
You cannot fast as you do today
and expect your voice to be heard
on high.'

'Is not this the kind of fasting I have
chosen:
to loose the chains of injustice
and untie the cords of the yoke,
to set the oppressed free
and break every yoke?
Is it not to share your food with the
hungry
and to provide the poor wanderer
with shelter —
when you see the naked, to clothe
him,

and not to turn away from your
own flesh and blood?
Then your light will break forth like
the dawn,
and your healing will quickly
appear;
then your righteousness will go
before you,
and the glory of the LORD *will be*
your rearguard.
Then you will call, and the LORD *will*
answer;
you will cry for help, and he will
say: Here am I.'
'If you do away with the yoke of
oppression,
with the pointing finger and
malicious talk,
and if you spend yourselves on
behalf of the hungry
and satisfy the needs of the
oppressed,
then your light will rise in the
darkness,
and the night will become like
the noonday.'

Isaiah 58: 3, 4, 6-10

Until recently I'd always thought of poverty as simply a lack of wealth — little money, few belongings, inadequate housing, and so on. But a visit to Haiti for a Tear Fund film project opened my eyes to a more basic definition. Poverty is an absence of choice.

Think about it. Most of us in this country are faced with all manner of choices from the time we get out of bed. What clothes to wear? What cereal for breakfast? Marmalade or peanut butter on the toast? Bus or car to the office? Which TV channel to watch in the evening? Home cooking or a Chinese take-away for dinner? Which album to buy? Which film to see? What to buy Mum for her birthday? It's endless. Life seems to be made up of decision-making, even though most of the time we don't realise it.

But for someone living in Haiti or in a drought-devastated area of Africa, or anywhere else in what we call the Third World, it's a different story. Basically there's only one choice of any significance — whether to live or die. Hard as it is to grasp, the majority of the world's population never have

the luxury of deciding what to eat, what to wear, what to buy, or where to go, because there are no options. You eat the grain and drink dubious water or you starve. You wear yesterday's rags or you go naked. You sit where you have always sat because there's nowhere else to go.

It's an unthinkable nightmare, and for me the contrast was starkly reinforced when we continued filming in a huge family amusement park in the south of England. Choice with a vengeance! Thirty-two ice-cream flavours. One hundred or more 'fun' experiences. Dozens of ways to spend your money.

I'm not critical of that recreation for kids — just ashamed that the gulf between our world and theirs is so appallingly great, and that the quality of my life and the quality of theirs bears no shred of resemblance. And I am challenged yet again by this warning from Isaiah that the formalities and rituals of religion are not worth a light unless they go hand in hand with a practical concern for the poor and oppressed — for those with no choice.

LORD OF THE WALLET!

*And now, brothers, we want you to
know about the grace that God has
given the Macedonian churches. Out of
the most severe trial, their overflowing
joy and their extreme poverty welled
up in rich generosity. For I testify that
they give as much as they were able,
and even beyond their ability.
Entirely on their own, they urgently
pleaded with us for the privilege of
sharing in this service to the saints.
And they did not do as we expected,
but they gave themselves first to the
Lord and then to us in keeping with
God's will. So we urged Titus, since he
had earlier made a beginning, to bring
also to completion this act of grace on
your part. But just as you excel in
everything — in faith, in speech, in
knowledge, in complete earnestness
and in your love for us — see that you
also excel in this grace of giving.*

*I am not commanding you, but I
want to test the sincerity of your love
by comparing it with the earnestness
of others.*

2 Corinthians 8: 1-8

It's difficult for me to express thoughts about generosity and giving because
I'm all too aware that I've got more cash in the bank than most.
Nevertheless, the principle of Christian giving applies equally to all of us,
whether we're hard up or wealthy, and generosity certainly isn't a privilege
of the rich.

Some of us seem incredibly inconsistent when it comes to giving cash to
God's work. On the one hand we claim to have given our lives to the Lord,
but we don't let Him have our wallets. We give time and energy, but only
10p to missionary work. We think nothing of spending pounds on a meal,
an album or a new outfit, while Jesus is left with the small change.

There are times, I know, when Christians can be fantastically generous.
I've seen some of the letters that accompany donations to Tear Fund, for
instance, and have been really moved by sacrifices that must have actually
hurt. Sometimes it seems that people stretch themselves beyond their
means or 'beyond their ability' as Paul says, and I'm sure when that
happens the Lord blesses the giver every bit as much as the gift.

It's perhaps the more mundane and routine giving to the church and, more specifically, to our needy friends and neighbours where most of us have to learn lessons. From early Old Testament days, God's people were required to present a tenth of their income and harvest to the synagogue. Sometimes it was more, but never less, than a tenth. Jesus never reduced that expectation and I suspect a lot of us will have our knuckles rapped one day for being disobedient and failing to help meet needs that were on our very doorstep.

I've told this story before but it taught me a lot and it's worth a repeat. Two nurses working in a shanty town area of Lisbon asked an old Christian man why he insisted on giving them half of all he earned. The old man was desperately poor, his home was literally a sheet of corrugated tin propped against a wall, and he earned the equivalent of a few pence a day, collecting and selling scrap paper.

The old gentleman looked at the nurses as if they should have known better than even to ask the question. 'There's two of us on the job — God and me', he said. 'So we split what we earn fifty-fifty.'

ALL RUBBISH!

If anyone else thinks he has reasons to put confidence in the flesh, I have more: circumcised on the eighth day, of the people of Israel, of the tribe of Benjamin, a Hebrew of Hebrews; in regard to the law, a Pharisee; as for zeal, persecuting the church; as for legalistic righteousness, faultless.

But whatever was to my profit I now consider loss for the sake of Christ. What is more, I consider everything a loss compared to the surpassing greatness of knowing Christ Jesus my Lord, for whose sake I have lost all things. I consider them rubbish, that I may gain Christ and be found in him, not having a righteousness of my own that comes from the law, but that which is through faith in Christ — the righteousness that comes from God and is by faith.

Philippians 3: 4b-9

'OK,' says Paul, 'so you think you're a pretty decent, law-abiding character. You do your bit for charity and keep in God's good books by looking in at church every so often. You've no skeletons in the cupboard — or none worth boasting about — and, all in all, secretly think that if other folk were more like you the world would be a better place. God ought to be well satisfied.

'Let me tell you, when it comes to point-scoring,' Paul goes on, 'compared to me you're not in the running. A five-star Jew, I've a track record second to none. Since a child I've observed every religious ceremony and ritual, and there's not a rule or regulation that I've ignored or disobeyed. I challenge you to find even one flaw. And, as for enthusiasm, everyone knows the lengths I've been to to stamp out the crowd I thought were God's enemies. Humanly speaking, I was the model of religious respectability and, if anyone had cause for sitting back and thinking he'd scored, it was me. Yet now I know that all that religion, all that fanaticism, all that strict living and clockwork attendance at the synagogue, amounted to absolute zilch. In God's sight it was, to coin a phrase, "a load of rubbish".

'Compared to knowing Jesus, that old life style amounted to nothing. By all that discipline and effort and law-keeping, I actually believed I could earn myself a place in God's family. I couldn't have been more wrong! Yesterday I had to face God with a qualification or a righteousness that was all down to me. Today I face Him with a righteousness that's been given to me by Jesus. There just ain't no comparison!'

Well, that was Paul's experience — with a pinch of author's licence. I know I've made the same point myself several times, about our own good deeds being insufficient in themselves, but I thought if you didn't believe me, you might listen to Paul!

BY SPECIAL INVITATION

'Come to me, all you who are weary and burdened, and I will give you rest. Take my yoke upon you and learn from me, for I am gentle and humble in heart, and you will find rest for your souls. For my yoke is easy and my burden is light.'

Matthew 11: 28-30

I'm not usually in the habit of hanging on to souvenirs and keepsakes. I suppose constant travel makes me a bit blasé, besides which my attic is already groaning under the weight of other assorted junk accumulated over the years.

One memento I can't bring myself to throw out, though, is an elegant gilt-edged card inviting me to Buckingham Palace, no less, for lunch with the Queen. Well, it isn't every day of the week that I get one of those, and the experience was unforgettable.

It was an invitation I couldn't refuse but, even so and with the utmost respect, it wasn't nearly as irresistible as the one given here by Jesus. You'll never receive an invitation sent with so much love, that's for sure, and it's offered not to a privileged few but to 'whosoever'. No conditions laid down, no qualifications, no formalities: 'Whoever needs me,' says Jesus, 'you come'.

In our high-pressure world, there are a whole lot of weary and burdened people. We all know what it's like when things get on top of us. One problem follows another and there seems no light at the end of the tunnel. We try various remedies; 'drink' is an escape route for some, and anti-depressants and tranquillisers are as routine in millions of homes as a morning cup of tea. But, try as we might to stifle the symptoms, there's nowhere to go to sort out the real cause of the mess. Except, that is, to Jesus, who invites us to submit to His authority and control. Not an oppressive dictatorial sort of control, which makes life an even greater drag, but one that's gentle, compassionate and for our good.

A yoke, I'm told, was one of those heavy wooden collars strung across the necks of working animals, like oxen. When the yoke was in position, the animal knew it was under the control of its owner and would be led obediently by every gentle tug and pull. But, whereas the ox's yoke was restricting and literally a weight around its neck, Jesus promises that His authority is light and easy.

When commitments and pressures and people get all a bit much for me — and quite often they do — I find tremendous comfort and relief in just bringing Jesus' invitation consciously to mind and responding to it with my will. The problems don't go, but they become far more bearable.

Like most invitations, by the way, the choice is ours to decline or accept.

PEOPLE IN GLASS HOUSES ...

But Jesus went to the Mount of Olives. At dawn he appeared again in the temple courts, where all the people gathered round him, and he sat down to teach them. The teachers of the law and the Pharisees brought in a woman caught in adultery. They made her stand before the group and said to Jesus, 'Teacher this woman was caught in the act of adultery. In the Law Moses commanded us to stone such women. Now what do you say?' They were using this question as a trap, in order to have a basis for accusing him.

But Jesus bent down and started to write on the ground with his finger. 'When they kept on questioning him,

he straightened up and said to them, 'If any one of you is without sin, let him be the first to throw a stone at her.' Again he stooped down and wrote on the ground.

At this, those who heard began to go away one at a time, the older ones first, until only Jesus was left, with the woman still standing there. Jesus straightened up and asked her, 'Woman, where are they? Has no-one condemned you?'

'No-one, sir,' she said.

'Then neither do I condemn you,' Jesus declared. 'Go now and leave your life of sin.'

John 8: 1-11

What a horrible tendency there is to zero in on people's faults rather than on their strengths. Sadly, it seems almost a preoccupation of some Christians to gossip about, knock, and even publicly denounce other Christians whose lives or opinions don't match up to their personal expectations. Take a look at the correspondence columns of Christian publications and you'll see what I mean. There's nothing wrong with open Christian debate and even controversy, but how miserable when that spills over into spiteful personal criticism. 'How dreadful of so-and-so to say that or do this or go there. How dare he call himself a Christian...' The appealing thing about fault-finding in others of course is that it keeps the focus away from our own deficiencies and disobedience, and helps us feel ever so self-righteous!

Jesus' encounter with the woman who'd committed adultery is such an eye-opener. There couldn't be two more opposing attitudes towards her. On the one hand, the uncaring Pharisees, who were only out to make a point. Preservation of their legalistic heartless doctrine was all that mattered. The

DISGRACEFUL - YOUR GRACE!

woman was just a convenient pawn to put Jesus on the spot. This time they had Him. The woman's welfare was irrelevant.

But not so for Jesus. With what must have been fantastically dramatic timing, He turned the tables on the Pharisees with that classic all-time debunking of hypocrisy. And the religious hoi-polloi slunk away. At least they were honest!

No, Jesus didn't say the woman's adultery didn't matter. If the Pharisees had stood their ground, they would have realised that Jesus was far from dismissing Moses' old law. It would be very convenient of course. 'Jesus loves us so we can do as we like.' But read the verses carefully. Obviously Jesus had tremendous compassion for that woman, and what she had done hadn't lessened His love for her in the slightest degree. There were no rebukes or threats, no indignant shock or uncomfortable embarrassment. Just as she was, she was loved and accepted. Only from now on she must change her ways. Now she had met Jesus, life had to be different. *She* was acceptable but her sin was not!

FLABBERGASTED!

So Peter was kept in prison, but the church was earnestly praying to God for him.

The night before Herod was to bring him to trial, Peter was sleeping between two soldiers, bound with two chains, and sentries stood guard at the entrance. Suddenly an angel of the Lord appeared and a light shone in the cell. He struck Peter on the side and woke him up. 'Quick, get up!' he said, and the chains fell off Peter's wrists.

Then the angel said to him, 'Put on your clothes and sandals.' And Peter did so. 'Wrap your cloak around you and follow me,' the angel told him. Peter followed him out of the prison, but he had no idea that what the angel was doing was really happening; he thought he was seeing a vision. They passed the first and second guards and came to the iron gate leading to the city. It opened for them by itself, and they went through it. When they had walked the length of one street,
suddenly the angel left him.

Then Peter came to himself and said, 'Now I know without a doubt that the Lord sent his angel and rescued me from Herod's clutches and from everything the Jewish people were anticipating.'

When this had dawned on him, he went to the house of Mary the mother of John, also called Mark, where many people had gathered and were praying. Peter knocked at the outer entrance, and a servant girl named Rhoda came to answer the door. When she recognised Peter's voice, she was so overjoyed she ran back without opening it and exclaimed, 'Peter is at the door!'

'You're out of your mind,' they told her. When she kept insisting that it was so, they said, 'It must be his angel.'

But Peter kept on knocking, and when they opened the door and saw him, they were astonished.

Acts 12: 5-16

You've got to smile! Just imagine it. Here were these dear earnest Christians, all fervently praying away for Peter's safety, while all the time he was waiting outside, banging the front door. Almost certainly they had been praying for a miracle, but when the maid told them Peter was free and was at the door they thought she was potty. Fancy interrupting their prayers with daft nonsense like that!

I'd love to have seen their faces when Peter eventually walked in. But, before we're too critical, it strikes me that their praying was absolutely typical of our own approach far too often. We ask God to heal or overrule in some situation, but in our heart of hearts we don't believe for a moment that He will. Or, to be more accurate, we're not convinced that He can! What we're asking for is too big, too impossible, too outlandish. Miracles are a bit like raffle prizes. They're things that happen to other people, not to us, and if we actually got what we asked for we'd be flabbergasted.

What a doubting crowd we are. We say we believe God answers prayer, but at the same time we wouldn't stake our lives on it! Obviously, from the evidence of this story, God still sometimes intervenes miraculously, despite a lack of total conviction from those who ask. There's little doubt that these Christians took their praying seriously and, despite their lack of optimism, God still honoured their obedience and faithfulness.

'... I tell you,' said Jesus to the disciples, 'whatever you ask for in prayer, believe that you have received it, and it will be yours.' (Mark 11:24).

Confidence like that is hard to practise. And there's always the possibility of course that our praying may not be in line with God's will. But God's ability to intervene is one thing; whether He chooses to is another.

HARD TO HANDLE

Who has believed our message
 and to whom has the arm of the LORD been revealed?
He grew up before him like a tender shoot,
 and like a root out of dry ground.
He had no beauty or majesty to attract us to him,
 nothing in his appearance that we should desire him.
He was despised and rejected by men,
 a man of sorrows, and familiar with suffering.
Like one from whom men hide their faces
 he was despised, and we esteemed him not.

Isaiah 53: 1-3

One of the hardest forms of mental anguish to cope with must be the feeling of rejection. To believe that, for one reason or another, you are unacceptable in the eyes of others must produce a dreadful and destructive isolation. There's even something pathetic about the items in a 'reject' shop. Despite the cheerful packaging, the stuff is different and separate from the rest. Not good enough, inferior, cheap.

Tragically, there are many in our community who see themselves in that category. Sometimes the causes are obvious. The out-of-work youngster who's applied for job after job, but no employer wants to know. After the tenth rejection slip, no wonder self-confidence gives way to self-doubt and pessimism. There's the Asian or West Indian who does his best to fit in with our society, but every day is snubbed, ignored, or insulted, for no other reason than being different. There's a limit to how tough-skinned you can be.

Sometimes the most painful rejection feelings come from more subtle causes. The boy or girl, for instance, who feels unwanted to unloved by selfish insensitive parents. The husband or wife whose partner suddenly finds another love. The elderly mother or father whose 'usefulness' seems to be over and feels only a burden and a nuisance. The homosexual who hates his unnatural tendencies but has nowhere to go for help or compassion. The disabled or disfigured who are conscious that society would prefer not even to look.

The list could go on and on. Maybe the biggest group of all are those who feel 'out of it' for no logical reason. All they know is that in a crowd they're the ones nobody seems interested in and no one talks to.

Whereas it's hard for me to say I know how you feel — because, in all honesty, I don't — there are many churches around nowadays which have expert and sympathetic counsellors ready to lend an ear and offer advice. I'd really urge you to take the initiative and make contact. Meanwhile, remember that Jesus understands more about isolation than anyone. When He yelled out from the cross, 'My God, why have you forsaken me?', I guess He must have felt the combined rejection of the whole of humanity, and the pain and enormity of that experience was greater than anything we'll ever know. But, although rejected Himself, no one was ever too bad, too inadequate or too unlovely for Jesus. Even the criminal on the next cross found acceptance in the assurance that 'today you will be with me in paradise'.

Of one thing then you can be absolutely certain. There's no way you're a reject as far as God is concerned. In His eyes you're unique, priceless, and totally acceptable just as you are, warts and all, job or no job. With that assurance it has to be easier to soldier on.

'WHATEVER YOU DO...'

Let the peace of Christ rule in your hearts, since as members of one body you were called to peace. And be thankful. Let the word of Christ dwell in you richly as you teach and admonish one another with all wisdom, and as you sing psalms, hymns and spiritual songs with gratitude in your hearts to God. And whatever you do, whether in word or deed, do it all in the name of the Lord Jesus, giving thanks to God the Father through him.

Colossians 3: 15-17

Here's a really useful principle to get engrained in our minds. It's the last sentence, about whatever we do being in the name of Jesus. Not just religious things, notice, like praying or going to church, but 'whatever you do' — in other words, everything. Washing up, homework, singing on stage, office filing — whatever. It's an important principle for three reasons, as far as I'm concerned.

One, it shows us that God doesn't divide life's activity into neat little compartments, some of which interest Him and some of which don't. We assume quite wrongly if we think God is more interested when we're praying than when we're hoovering, or more attentive when we're singing a hymn than hitting a tennis ball. God is interested and involved in all we do, and that division between secular and sacred is of our own making; it is no part of New Testament teaching. 'The only thing that is secular,' I heard a preacher say, 'is sin'.

That brings me to point two (I feel like a school-teacher!).

If ever you are in doubt about the 'rightness' of any action, ask yourself whether you're comfortable about doing it 'in the name of Jesus'. Need I say more? You'll know the answer without anyone else's advice.

And, thirdly, can you imagine how much improved the quality of life would be if we were all motivated to do our work and play our games and build our relationships in the name of Jesus? Wouldn't we do everything that much better, because in Jesus' name nothing can be less than the very best? For sure, it would do away with the grasping philosophy that preaches minimum effort for maximum reward. The Christian way is maximum effort for a maximum sacrifice — and we're grateful!

ONE THING I KNOW

The Jews still did not believe that he had been blind and had received his sight until they sent for the man's parents. 'Is this your son?' they asked. 'Is this the one you say was born blind? How is it that now he can see?'

'We know he is our son,' the parents answered, 'and we know he was born blind. But how he can see now, or who opened his eyes, we don't know. Ask him. He is of age; he will speak for himself.' His parents said this because they were afraid of the Jews, for

already the Jews had decided that anyone who acknowledged that Jesus was the Christ would be put out of the synagogue. That was why his parents said, 'He is of age; ask him.'

A second time they summoned the man who had been blind. 'Give glory to God,' they said. 'We know this man is a sinner.'

He replied, 'Whether he is a sinner or not, I don't know. One thing I do know, I was blind but now I see!'

John 9: 18-25

You can almost feel the exasperation. Jesus' healing of the blind man had caused an uproar and questions were being fired from every direction. How did it happen? Is it a set-up? Was the blind guy switched for someone else? Will it last? Can he really see?

Today it would be the cynical and sensation-seeking media; then it was Jesus' enemies and a curious, incredulous crowd. And the man who was healed, and his parents, were nearly overwhelmed by the sudden attention and demands. Besides that, most of the questions were impossible. How do you explain a miracle? 'I don't know,' said the man; 'all I can tell you is that once I was blind, but now I can see.' And to everyone who watched, pop-eyed and open-mouthed, the change was obvious.

Two thousand years later the world is even more sceptical and suspicious of what it doesn't understand, and yet still the miracles of healed bodies and changed lives won't go away. I've referred to healing miracles elsewhere and I'm convinced that God still does intervene to restore and cure where medicine sometimes fails. Why He does so in some instances and not others, I don't know — just as I've no idea why Jesus restored the sight of this man and left hundreds of others He must have met still blind.

But the commotion in this story reminds me of reaction to people's conversion just as much as to life-changing miracles. How did it happen? Was it the powerful speaker? Will it wear off? Is it psychological?

Be sure of one thing. When people notice a difference, the questions will flow thick and fast. They may be cynical. They may intend to catch us out. They may just be healthily curious. I think back to my own conversion and, like all the other countless testimonies from Christians around the world, I can only make a simple statement. I have no scientific explanation for what happened, and no mathematical formula. All I know is that spiritually once I was blind; now I can see. The only proof I can offer is a life that's changed — and you can see that for yourself.

READY FOR THE CROWN

For I am already being poured out like a drink offering, and the time has come for my departure. I have fought the good fight, I have finished the race, I have kept the faith. Now there is in store for me the crown of righteousness, which the Lord, the righteous Judge, will award to me on that day — and not only to me, but also to all who have longed for his appearing.

2 Timothy 4: 6-8

How fantastic to be able to approach death with this sort of calm confidence! I know that dying is a subject most of us prefer not to dwell on. Better to cross that bridge when we come to it, we say, and even sensible preparation, like making a will, is put off because somehow it's morbid!

Not so for Paul. He was so sure of what the Lord had in store for him, so confident of God's promises, that he was actually looking forward to it. I've met some who think it's wrong to presume a place in heaven. 'We can only hope,' they say, 'that if there's a God then we'll make it. To be certain of getting there is just arrogant.'

Not necessarily of course, because it all depends where we've put our confidence. If it's in our 'good works' or in our gifts to charity or in our kindness to animals and to old ladies, then that certainly is misplaced. If, on the other hand, it's in Jesus and in what He has done and said, then our entry visa to heaven is dependent on Him, with no self-credit whatsoever.

To know that we don't deserve even one tiny jewel of this 'crown of righteousness' which is being prepared for us cannot result in arrogance, surely, only a grateful humility.

Note that Paul doesn't say he won the fight or came first in the race. The point is that he took part and finished. Goodness knows how many times he may have crashed flat on his back or how often he stumbled and fell. That didn't matter, because God wasn't keeping count.

It's a lovely reassuring thought that God doesn't demand one hundred per cent success rate from His family. I'm sure He would be over the moon, so to speak, if we achieved it but He knows we can't. What He asks is that, despite the setbacks and the disappointments, we keep going and, even though on points the verdict should warrant a 'thumbs down', and though we've been lapped a hundred times by those seeming to be in life's fast lane, the only judge who has any clout is God. And He's already got the winner's medal beautifully polished and with our name indelibly inscribed.

AGONY AUNT

Brothers, if someone is caught in a sin, you who are spiritual should restore him gently. But watch yourself, or you also may be tempted. Carry each other's burdens, and in this way you will fulfil the law of Christ. If anyone thinks he is something when he is nothing, he deceives himself. Each one should test his own actions. Then he can take pride in himself, without comparing himself to somebody else, for each one should carry his own load.

Galatians 6: 1-5

Here's a recipe for those suffering with inflated egos, and a Yorkshireman couldn't be more blunt. I guess we can all think of plenty of people who would fit nicely into the 'cat's whiskers' category. People we don't much like, probably, who put on airs and graces, and think a darn sight too much of themselves. We all know them.

But hold on! Paul says, 'watch yourself'. He's talking about you and me and is being very personal. Let's not fob off the challenge by doing what comes easily and picking holes in others. This time *we're* under scrutiny. But before jumping to conclusions we need to see the context of Paul's warning. Inevitably Christians will find themselves from time to time in a position where they have to counsel and give advice to other people. They may not seek to and may not even want to, but if someone is known to have convinced Christian faith it's surprising how frequently he or she is the one that others turn to automatically for help or comfort. Just occasionally the situation may crop up where a Christian feels he has to be quite 'heavy' with someone and say, 'Look, what you're doing or what you're thinking is wrong and is going to cause you or someone else to be hurt. Sort yourself out.'

The advice may be right, but we're on dangerous ground because it's so easy for that smug 'holier than thou' attitude to creep in and wipe out all our potential usefulness with one stroke.

'Watch out,' says Paul. If you're advising others on how to live, don't let their mistakes or their weaknesses cause you to think you're any better. There is only one person that Christians must measure up to and that's Jesus. Against Him those of us who quietly regard ourselves as 'quite something' may be shocked to discover that we're 'absolutely nothing'.

As long as we remember that, we could well be surprised and grateful at just how effective a helper and counsellor we can be.

JUST GOOD FRIENDS

The LORD detests lying lips,
  but he delights in men who are truthful.
A prudent man keeps his knowledge to himself,
  but the heart of fools blurts out folly.
Diligent hands will rule,
  but laziness ends in slave labour.
An anxious heart weighs a man down,
  but a kind word cheers him up.
A righteous man is cautious in friendship,
  but the way of the wicked leads them astray.

Proverbs 12:22-26

More little nuggets of wisdom from Proverbs, but it's the last one, about being 'cautious in friendship', that caught my eye. Maybe I've a bigger circle of acquaintances than most, and with every tour I go on that circle tends to expand more. My Christmas card list would be ridiculous if I sent to everyone I was friendly with! But there's a difference between acquaintances and friends, and even between 'being friendly' and actual friendship.

It may surprise you, but I probably don't have many more real friends than the ordinary reader, and most of them, although not all, tend to be outside show-business. Friends, for me, tend to be the people I choose to spend most time with or, if distance makes that impossible, they're the ones I can relate to most easily and naturally even after many months of absence.

Today most of my friends, although again not all, tend to be Christians. Men and women who share the same love and enthusiasm and priorities that I have. And I couldn't really imagine it any other way. Close friendship implies like minds and a common understanding, which enable mutual support and encouragement. For me I think it would be impossible to find that outside the Christian 'family'.

There's a lot of truth, I reckon, in the old saying about being known by the friends we keep. Whether we admit it or not, our friends do have enormous influence on our lives, particularly when we're young. To be simplistic about it, it's easier to be good in the company of some people, and it's easier to be bad in the company of others!

I wonder what path my life would have taken if I hadn't met, mixed with and befriended a group of very ordinary Christian guys way back in the mid-sixties. Their influence caused me to open my life to Christ and His influence changed me.

My advice then to any young Christian is to go out of your way to ensure that your best mates are Christians too. When one of you falls down, there's a guarantee of someone close by to give a hand up.

The flip-side of that advice is that Christians shouldn't be exclusive with their friendships. If *all* your friends are Christians, then you've gone overboard in the other direction and wiped out for yourself one of the most strategic channels of witness and evangelism.

Do a quick count now. List all your friends — real friends — and check the balance.

NO FAVOURITES

My brothers, as believers in our glorious Lord Jesus Christ, don't show favouritism. Suppose a man comes into your meeting wearing a gold ring and fine clothes, and a poor man in shabby clothes also comes in. If you show special attention to the man wearing fine clothes and say, 'Here's a good seat for you,' but say to the poor man, 'You stand there,' or 'Sit on the floor by my feet,' have you not discriminated among yourselves and become judges with evil thoughts?

Listen my dear brothers: Has not God chosen those who are poor in the eyes of the world to be rich in faith and to inherit the kingdom he promised those who love him?

James 2: 1-5

Most of us, I guess, are a bit snobbish when it comes to other people's appearance. If we don't like the look of the guy with orange hair and a stud in his nose, then we don't fall over backwards to be friendly. Very different though for the well-heeled blonde with the attractive smile!

Now obviously our human 'chemistry' causes us to react to people in different ways. We are automatically drawn to some people and the vibes seem to click immediately, while others, frankly, are a pain in the neck.

Chemistry is one thing. Blatant snobbery is another. When we see it operating in society it's ugly and demeaning. When it occurs within the church it's inexcusable. Christians are required to be different, and that difference must be evident, most of all in the way we react to and treat others. Appearances are deceptive, we know that, and of course we grew up with the old proverb, 'All that glitters is not gold'. Yet how automatic it still is to judge a person's value by their clothing, hairstyle, cleanliness, or even accent or colour of skin. 'Does this look or sound like someone I'd like to know?' we subconsciously ask ourselves. 'Is this person likely to be any use to me?' Those are the criteria that determine whether we put ourselves out or give the bare minimum; whether we care or cut dead.

For the Christian, such a self-centred and calculating yardstick is definitely out of order. What is relevant now is not my jaundiced assessment, but God's valuation. I have to remember that everyone, irrespective of their outward appearance or cultural background, is made in God's image and is the target of His love. There are no exceptions, no matter how unlovely to look at or to be near, no matter how socially unacceptable or disgraced, no matter how much a failure or a fool. God's love is shared equally among all His creatures, and Jesus died not for a social elite but for the whole world.

As a Christian then, I have to reflect His undiscriminating love. It goes against the grain and I can't pretend I don't make hasty biased judgments, but it's yet another area of Christian living where I have to press on and, from a combination of my commitment and God's remarkable ability to change even the most stubborn parts of my personality, become just a little more Christ-like.

OUTSIDE OF TIME

But do not forget this one thing, dear friends: With the Lord a day is like a thousand years, and a thousand years are like a day. The Lord is not slow in keeping his promise, as some understand slowness. He is patient with you, not wanting anyone to perish, but everyone to come to repentance.

But the day of the Lord will come like a thief. The heavens will disappear with a roar; the elements will be destroyed by fire, and the earth and everything in it will be laid bare.

Since everything will be destroyed in this way, what kind of people ought you to be? You ought to live holy and godly lives as you look forward to the day of God and speed its coming. That day will bring about the destruction of the heavens by fire, and the elements will melt in the heat. But in keeping with his promise we are looking forward to a new heaven and a new earth, the home of righteousness.

2 Peter 3: 8-13

We've already looked at another part of the Bible where Jesus' return to this world is predicted as an absolute certainty. No dates are announced, but the principle is beyond dispute. One day the Lord will intervene directly and dramatically in the world's affairs and, to put it mildly, there'll be a few changes around the place!

The key question of course is when. Although it's easy to grasp the idea that He'll come suddenly and unexpectedly, two thousand years of uninterrupted history seems a heck of a long time! All through the ages people have been saying that His coming was imminent, only to end up with the odd smear of egg on their faces. It's natural that, in view of such prolonged unfulfilled expectation, some will grow impatient and cynical. Maybe the Lord's forgotten and changed His mind! A bunch of curious theologians even volunteered the theory that God had died and the world was now, presumably, careering pointlessly to who knows what conclusion.

I find Peter's reminder at the start of this passage really helpful. Whereas we, as it were, are trapped within time, and ideas like time-warps and travel across history belong to the likes of Dr Who, God exists outside the limitations of minutes and hours. And, although I don't understand that, I have to accept that God is greater than my puny little mind, and Peter's explanation that, as far as God is concerned, a day is no different to a thousand years (and vice versa) makes good sense.

In the same way, whether He returns in my lifetime or in some remote future century makes little difference to my Christian life now. The point is that some day I must face Him and be accountable.

As a little footnote, it's worth pondering that the second coming of Jesus is one of the few remaining major Bible prophecies that has yet to come true. The rest have proved remarkably and compellingly accurate!

NO PUSHOVER

When it was daylight, the magistrates sent their officers to the jailer with the order: 'Release those men.' The jailer told Paul, 'The magistrates have ordered that you and Silas be released. Now you can leave. Go in peace.'

But Paul said to the officers: 'They beat us publicly without a trial, even though we are Roman citizens, and threw us into prison. And now do they want to get rid of us quietly? No! Let them come themselves and escort us out.'

The officers reported this to the magistrates, and when they heard that Paul and Silas were Roman citizens, they were alarmed. They came to appease them and escorted them from the prison, requesting them to leave the city. After Paul and Silas came out of the prison, they went to Lydia's house, where they met with the brothers and encouraged them. Then they left.

Acts 16: 35-40

I don't think I'd want to be on the wrong side of Paul. He certainly wasn't the kind of guy who suffered fools gladly and, as these civil servants discovered, you pushed him around at your peril! I can imagine the magistrates' red faces and embarrassed apologies as they tried to smooth things over with the minimum fuss. They knew only too well that, if Paul chose, he could make life distinctly awkward for them. Career prospects would be out of the window, to say the least! To ignore the rights and privileges of two Roman citizens was a blunder of the first order.

I wonder if Paul's attitude surprises you. Maybe you'd have expected him to hurry away from the prison at the first opportunity. After all, it wasn't exactly a health farm. Instead of that, he stubbornly stayed put until the magistrates appeared in person, offered profuse apologies, and invited him to leave. Rubbing their noses in the dirt, you might say.

Maybe so, but there's nothing in the Bible to suggest that Christians must be weak-kneed ninnies. Meekness isn't the same as weakness, and 'turning the other cheek' doesn't mean we offer ourselves as Aunt Sallies to every

character who'd enjoy taking a swipe. Too often Christian love has been misconstrued as a feeble 'niceness' and something to take advantage of and manipulate.

When Jesus turfed those money-changers out of the Temple, scattered their cash, and upturned their tables, it certainly wasn't 'nice'. Hardly gentle and loving, and by no means courteous. But in the circumstances it was right. The money-changers would hardly have packed up and left if Jesus had asked them 'nicely'. They needed firm handling — and they got it.

There's nothing virtuous in letting yourself be walked over. It brings no respect to you or the Lord. Sometimes it may be necessary to dig your heels in over a principle, and even to be a downright nuisance. I well remember bringing legal action against a national music paper for an incredibly offensive 'review' of one of my gospel concerts.

Mind you, you need to be sure the cause is right and that you aren't merely defending your own bruised ego. Sometimes it needs a lot of wisdom to tell the difference.

BEFORE AND AFTER

Since, then, you have been raised with Christ, set your hearts on things above, where Christ is seated at the right hand of God. Set your minds on things above, not on earthly things. For you died, and your life is now hidden with Christ in God. When Christ, who is your life, appears, then you also will appear with him in glory.

Put to death, therefore, whatever belongs to your earthly nature: sexual immorality, impurity, lust, evil desires and greed, which is idolatry.

Because of these, the wrath of God is coming. You used to walk in these ways, in the life you once lived. But now you must rid yourselves of all such things as these: anger, rage, malice, slander and filthy language from your lips. Do not lie to each other, since you have taken off your old self with its practices and have put on the new self, which is being renewed in knowledge in the image of its Creator.

Colossians 3: 1-10

Old and new, before and after, dead and alive. If you wonder whether Christianity makes that much difference, Paul really lays it on the line. 'Once your life was like this,' he says; 'now it's all changed'. Or has it? Maybe not as much as you'd wish, and some of the failings on Paul's blacklist give the conscience an uncomfortable tweak.

Don't be too discouraged, because Christians aren't immune from falling flat on their faces from time to time, and when they do the only answer is to get up, dust off, and keep walking, knowing the further and longer they walk, the surer their step and the firmer their foothold.

There are two 'before and after' images here, which helped me quite a bit in realising what a radical change there has been in me — even though I don't always make it apparent. Firstly, there's the idea of our old self having 'died' when we became Christians and our new life being completely wrapped up in Jesus. That means that all the unchristian 'left-overs' are no more than intruders in our new character and we should recognise them as such. They have no place in our lives any longer, and certainly no right to control us. God regards them as belonging to the past, and that's where we should relegate them too.

Then there's the idea of our old nature being taken off and discarded like a shabby overcoat. We wore it for a time — perhaps for too long — but now it's been chucked out and it's gone for ever. In its place is a brand new garment, totally restyled and different. We feel far better in it, that's for sure, and people say it suits us down to the ground. How daft to pretend, and behave as though we're still ragamuffins!

When I read these verses through a few times, five words stood out and stuck in my mind: 'You used to ... But now ...' What a difference!

IT HAS TO BE TRUE

'I have much more to say to you, more than you can now bear. But when he, the Spirit of truth, comes, he will guide you into all truth. He will not speak on his own; he will speak only what he hears, and he will tell you what is yet to come. He will bring glory to me by taking from what is mine and making it known to you. All that belongs to the Father is mine. That is why I said the Spirit will take from what is mine and make it known to you.'

John 16: 12-15

Some folks, I suspect, are too clever for their own good. I know I've only got two 'O' levels and have sung some pretty daft lyrics in my time, but I reckon I've a fair ration of common sense. I remember discussing religion once with a musician friend of mine, who was dabbling around with Buddhism and various fairly obscure Eastern philosophies. After about an hour of heavy chat, in which I tried to spell out my beliefs, he suddenly agreed. 'OK, you may be right.' I was just thinking, 'Great, we're getting somewhere', when he added, 'But then so might I be right. So might the Moslem and the Baha'i believer and the spiritualist. We might all be right. On the other hand, we might all be wrong! As long as you're sincere, it really doesn't matter.'

Now I don't know about you, but I can't cope with that. Sincerity doesn't necessarily equate with truth. It's often been pointed out that Hitler was sincere!

To my mind, something is either true — positively and objectively — or it isn't. Jesus and His good news is either true, and therefore reliable, relevant and vital for everyone — or it's the opposite. There can't be anything in-between. There are no degrees of truth; it's all or nothing.

I know it's easy to get bogged down in all sorts of intellectual and philosophical arguments from which you end up proving that black is white, or that the chair I'm sitting on isn't really there at all! Clever, no doubt, but a mind like that must have awful difficulty in grasping a faith which, according to Jesus, needs the simple approach of a child.

Why do I believe, and why should you? Not because it makes us feel good and gives us a warm glow. Not because it's an insurance policy for when we die. Not for anything we might get out of it — although that's immense. We should believe because it is true. It's as simple and basic as that. The result of a faith that is anchored to truth is that our relationship with God doesn't depend on our digestion, or the state of our current romance. God is the same on our good days, as well as the bad. Fact, not fiction.

JUST SUPPOSE ...

This grace was given us in Christ Jesus before the beginning of time, but it has now been revealed through the appearing of our Saviour, Christ Jesus, who has destroyed death and has brought life and immortality to light through the gospel. And of this gospel I was appointed a herald and an apostle and a teacher. That is why I am suffering as I am. Yet I am not ashamed, because I know whom I have believed, and am convinced that he is able to guard what I have entrusted to him for that day.

2 Timothy 1: 9b-12

Words like 'perhaps', 'possibly', 'if' and 'maybe' don't seem to feature much in Paul's vocabulary. If you check through all he wrote, you'll find precious little hesitation or um-ing and ah-ing. As he writes here, he knew his Lord and was convinced of His ability.

Doubts and misgivings will assault most of us from time to time, playing havoc with our determination to be one of Christ's fighters. They sap our confidence and cause us to question whether it's really worthwhile sticking our necks out. 'Suppose it's all a con or some wild fantasy?' 'Suppose Jesus wasn't who He said He was and when you die it's just, well, the end?' 'Suppose it's just every man for himself?' Common enough questions, I guess, but it's a shame if they linger around and undermine our usefulness.

Personally, I don't think they need linger and, although I appreciate that Paul had the distinct advantage of having that miraculous encounter with Jesus on the Damascus road that would have surely made a lasting impression on the most sceptical, there's ample foundation for us to be every bit as sure and convinced as he was. After all, we have the benefit of nearly two thousand years of Christian history to look back on. We have a complete Bible and vastly more knowledge and understanding of our universe and its incredible complexity, and there's archaeology and ancient records and brilliant scholarship, all of which point to the authenticity of Jesus and the Bible manuscript.

And, putting a seal on all the academic evidence — and the only factor really that will set us ablaze with enthusiasm — is our own experience of Jesus and the Holy Spirit in our lives. While others will need to see tangible evidence of His life in us, we can *know* His presence just as surely as Paul did and be just as convinced that He'll complete what He has begun.

Two reminders! Being sure and convinced isn't the same as being smug and arrogant. Avoid that kind of 'know-it-all' attitude at all costs. It's a guaranteed switch-off as far as friends and colleagues are concerned.

Secondly, people are fed up with woolly 'can't be sure of anything' Christianity. What is needed is quiet certainty and gentle conviction. That's winsome.

NEVER ALONE

I lift up my eyes to the hills —
  where does my help come from?
My help comes from the LORD,
  the Maker of heaven and earth.
He will not let your foot slip —
  he who watches over you will not slumber;
indeed, he who watches over Israel
  will neither slumber nor sleep.
The LORD watches over you —
  the LORD is your shade at your right hand;
the sun will not harm you by day,
  nor the moon by night.
The LORD will keep you from all harm —
  he will watch over your life;
the LORD will watch over your coming and going
  both now and for evermore.

Psalm 121

What a perfect prescription for someone who's lonely and afraid. The promise from God that He is constantly in control, never off-duty and never preoccupied.

Our tendency is to lumber God with human limitations and frailties. Because we get tired, fed up and intolerant, we assume He does too. Because we're snowed under with work and pressures, we reason that God too must be driven frantic by the welter of demands and priorities. How can He possibly find time for us? That's how we think and that's why we doubt.

Sometimes we distort God even further and imagine Him as a harsh demanding disciplinarian, who would fry us with a bolt of lightning if we so much as put a foot wrong. And then there's the *Star Wars* God — some remote impersonal force who set everything in motion and then abandoned it to its own crazy chaos. If that's what God is, then He's of little relevance and certainly doesn't match up to the God I know.

What a far cry from the truth, and from this tender and beautiful insight into God's character. If only we could be more aware that God was this close — always watching, caring and protecting, never letting anyone or anything come between us and His love. No need then for that awful tormenting loneliness and those irrational but crippling fears of the unknown. Instead it becomes possible to enjoy a peace, a quiet confidence and a deep sense of security that, in Paul's words, 'passes all understanding'.

A MATTER OF CHOICE

'Now fear the LORD and serve him with all faithfulness. Throw away the gods your forefathers worshipped beyond the River and in Egypt, and serve the LORD. But if serving the LORD seems undesirable to you, then choose for yourselves this day whom you will serve, whether the gods your forefathers served beyond the River, or the gods of the Amorites, in whose land you are living. But as for me and my household, we will serve the LORD.'

Joshua 24: 14-15

Joshua wasn't one for beating about the bush. He'd been through some hairy old experiences as leader of the Hebrew people, and now he was approaching the end of his days. For years the Jews had pussyfooted about with God, sometimes pleading for His help, at other times turning their backs on Him and worshipping some foreign idol. Enough was enough. Now it was time for straight talking and deliberate decisions. Like it or not, the people had to commit themselves. It was either God, who had delivered them from Egypt, or the idols and superstitions they'd encountered on their journey. They must serve one or the other, and the choice was theirs.

Some of us are in urgent need of that kind of up-front Joshua-type challenge. I'm all for thinking through the implications of Christian commitment, and I well remember that it took me three years to ask all my questions and ponder the answers. Only then did I make a decision. But there's a danger that we Christians make it all too casual, and water down the urgency of decision-making when sharing the gospel with other people. 'Think about it,' we say. 'Read a book. Get some advice.' That's good for some, but there may be others reading these words who need to be bashed straight between the eyes and made to realise that they've faffed around for long enough. They've neither believed or disbelieved, neither been a Christian nor an atheist. Like a child with a plaything, they've toyed with God when it suited them, and abandoned Him at the slightest distraction. Now there's a crossroads in life and playtime's over. It's time for commitment.

Very rarely does Christian experience materialise out of the blue. We're not born into it and we don't stumble over it unawares. In nine cases out of ten, it's the result of a deliberate and conscious choice. We may not understand all the implications at the time, but we know we have to serve someone in life, and the options are all too plain.

Rationally and unemotionally, just like Joshua, I would encourage you with all my heart to choose this day — right now — to serve Christ. You have the freedom of course to choose differently, but choose you must.

WHAT A BAND!

*Praise the L*ORD
Praise God in his sanctuary;
praise him in his mighty heavens.
Praise him for his acts of power;
praise him for his surpassing greatness.
Praise him with the sounding of the trumpet,
praise him with the harp and lyre,
praise him with tambourine and dancing,
praise him with the strings and flute,
praise him with the clash of cymbals,
praise him with resounding cymbals.
*Let everything that has breath praise the L*ORD

*Praise the L*ORD

Psalm 150

So that includes you. See you in the choir!

BIBLE INDEX